£1 00

G000229646

POPULAR DOGS' BREED SERIES

To Sunny and Harry, wherever they may be.
They were to have been the future.

Contents

Illustrations

IN THE TEXT

Introduction

To write about a breed which we have known and loved for over twenty-five years, a breed we have seen develop from obscurity to world-wide fame, can only be a pleasure and a labour of love. This book started as a text book, which we hoped would be an aid to newcomers to the Rottweiler, and a source of interest and perhaps debate to those, and there are now many, who have like us grown to know and love Rottweilers. As it developed we realized that it was becoming a testament and perhaps a philosophy of the Rottweiler. This is rightly so. The Rottweiler is not as other dogs. There are aspects of his character which make him unique. No other breed arouses such a desire for knowledge of all aspects of the dog by the ordinary domestic pet owner and by serious breeders. Many people own a dog: they love it, enjoy it and care for it. Rottweiler owners demand and need to know far more about their chosen breed than this. We hope that this book will help to provide this additional knowledge.

You will find that we frequently refer to the Rottweiler as male when, in fact, we could be speaking of either male or female. This is in no way male chauvinism. To refer repeatedly to 'him or her' becomes clumsy and any one who knows the Rottweiler will appreciate that they have far too much character to be described as 'it'.

Do not assume that Rottweiler bitches are in any way a subordinate group. In our experience, Rottweilers are a matriarchal society. The oldest bitch remains the respected senior citizen deferred to not only by other bitches but also by all the males. She retains her position by sheer mental domination even when far too old to assert herself physically.

We would like to express our gratitude to Mrs Sybil Harper who has spent many long hours struggling to convert illegible handwriting into typewritten copy. She has also given us the benefit of her years of experience as an owner, trainer and breeder of Rottweilers.

Our thanks are also due to Mr Peter Stone, whose dog interests lie today with another breed but whose past experience with Rottweilers, skill as an artist and patience with ourselves, produced the line drawings used in this book.

Finally, our thanks to all those too numerous to mention who over the years have given us photographs and told us Rottweiler anecdotes, many of which are used in this book.

Without these helpers the book would not have been so easy to write.

1

Origin and Development
of the Rottweiler

If one loves a breed, and those who devote most of their life
to one can usually claim to do so, there are two attractive
alternative claims as to its origin which one may make.
Firstly, that one created the breed oneself, a privilege given
to very few in this world. Secondly that it has a long and
ancient history. Many breed enthusiasts like to assert that
their breed's ancestors are carved on the Pyramids or pain-
ted on some prehistoric cave wall. The favourite Rottweiler
legend is that it crossed the Alps with the Romans. Certainly
we believe that some of the Rottweiler ancestors were
known to the Romans and that if you had marched with the
legions some two thousand years ago along the passes
through the Alps, then, between the masses of marching
men, guarding and shepherding the ill-disciplined rabble of
baggage animals and cattle, you would certainly have seen a
big, rough-coated, powerful dog playing his part in the
march of history. However, to describe this dog as the ances-
tor of the Rottweiler is about as accurate as saying that the
men who marched with him were among the ancestors of
today's Europeans. The dog we are talking about is best described as the 'mastiff type', which to most of us describes a
large, powerful dog, short in muzzle with a pronounced
stop. We should, however, point out that this is a simplified
categorization and that the experts will tell you that the
mastiff group includes breeds ranging from St Bernards
through some gundogs to bulldogs and even to Pekinese.
The general opinion is that the mastiff first came from the
Himalayas and spread from there across the Middle East and
into Southern and Western Europe. While many give credit
to the Romans for the spread of the mastiff around the
Mediterranean and up into Western Europe there are others

who point out that a mastiff-type skull dating from the Ice Age has been discovered in the London area, a similar one from Germany has been dated around 700 BC and France has produced similar specimens. The Celts had large war dogs and about 200 BC large British fighting dogs were recorded as being successful in the Roman circuses. It does not seem beyond the bounds of possibility that large, powerful, mastiff-type dogs originated in different areas at approximately the same time for the very valid reason that man in all these areas found that he had a need for such a dog and proceeded to develop it. What does seem certain is that dog breeders, as such, go further back in history than any of the breeds which they have produced. So unless your interest is natural history rather than the Rottweiler, we suggest that you leave the origin of your breed to those whose talents lie in pursuing rather vague and conflicting theories and start your study of the breed from its nameplace, the town of Rottweil, to the east of the Black Forest in Southern Germany.

The town of Rottweil goes back to the year 73 or 74 AD when the Roman Eleventh Legion laid out a camp on the bank of the river Neckar in Southern Germany. It rapidly became a major base camp and communication centre, eventually achieving the status of an Imperial Roman City and the title of Arae Flaviae. The Romans were driven out in AD 260 by the Alemanni. However, the area continued to be important as a provincial centre. From the red colour of its roof tiles and bricks it received the first half of its name, 'rot', while its origin as a Roman city gave it 'wil' for villa. So from the red-roofed Roman villa evolved the name Rottweil. By the thirteenth century the town on the hill on the left bank of the river had become a free city and an important trade centre for grain and livestock. Although much of it is now a modern city the older part still has the charm and style which allow it to be described as like a collection of cuckoo clocks.

Certainly here, as elsewhere along the roads of the Romans, were to be found the descendants of those big guard dogs which protected their masters and their cattle. These powerful working dogs had gradually spread along the line of march making their homes in the farms and villages. It is perhaps a charming fantasy to think of a dog posted on sentry duty, slipping away from his post for a tryst with a willing bitch in the nearby village and then creeping back before his absence is discovered. A story any soldier would understand. High in the mountain valleys, each locality tended to develop dogs to suit their tastes and needs. The difficulties of travel outside a limited area meant that type became firmly fixed. These mountain valleys have given us, in addition to the Rottweiler, many of the breeds we know today: the Pyrenean, the Swiss and the Bernese Mountain Dogs, the St Bernard and the lesser known Appenzeller and Entlebucher. In general these breeds have a harsh, thick, weather-resistant coat, sturdy body and, apart from the Appenzeller and Entlebucher which are medium, are of above average size. These are breeds which have been developed for the needs of a peasant economy, a general purpose animal able to drive and guard cattle but equally able as a hunting dog, a household guard, a draught dog or a pet.

The herding and guarding of cattle, sheep and other stock was a major function of the dog in a peasant economy. Fiennes and Fiennes in *The Natural History of the Dog*, 1968, point out that there is often confusion between the 'sheep herd' dogs and the 'shepherd dogs'. While the function of the 'sheep herd' was to drive and control stock, the 'shepherd dog' had as his prime purpose the duty of safeguarding the stock from marauders both human and otherwise. The thrifty peasant farmer who developed the Rottweiler looked for a dog who could combine both functions.

Rottweil, as we have said, developed as an important trade centre for grain and livestock. Buyers and sellers of cattle are said to have come from as far afield as France and Hungary. The cattle trade encouraged the development of the Rottweiler and from the Middle Ages onwards the name Rottweiler or Rottweil Butcher's Dog came to be applied to a dog not dissimilar from that which we know today. His need to control cattle, including dangerous bulls, probably meant that somewhere along the line dogs of the bulldog or *bullenbeisser* type were brought into the strain to give that massive jaw structure which today gives the Rottweiler such a powerful bite.

To a butcher looking for a working dog, it was immaterial

what colour his dog was, and for much of his early life the Rottweiler wore a much less stylized coat than he does today. His colour often included a white collar, white feet and white spots and patches. Even today many puppies are born with that little spot of white on the chest. In passing, a very well-known German Rottweiler judge, whose father had owned the breed for some forty years, told us that his father always picked a puppy with the white chest spot as he considered them to be more intelligent and trainable. Even overall colour showed much variation and included, in addition to the black and tan which we know, brown, blue striped with tan markings, and wolf grey with tan markings. As far as one can ascertain, whatever the main body colour, the tan markings were present in the same positions as on today's Rottweilers. The dog also tended to come in two sizes, big heavy dogs as draught animals and lighter smaller animals for herding. Heredity being what it is, these two sizes of the same breed occasionally manifest themselves today.

Roughly one hundred years ago dogs that came fairly close to what we understand as the Rottweiler today began to be seen. At the same time their *raison d'être* had virtually ceased to exist. Draught dogs were little used; in some countries their use had become illegal. Cattle were no longer driven long distances on the hoof. Numbers declined and it began to look as if the Rottweiler, like other old soldiers, would fade away. Fortunately the fame of the breed's qualities had spread far beyond its area of origin. At the same time interest in dogs for their own sake had begun to develop. Breeders began to appear whose interest was in improving and purifying breeds so that they bred true to a laid down standard. The dog ceased to be something bred purely for its working ability with little regard for what we call breed points. Instead breeders set out to codify, by means of a standard, the physical and mental characteristics of their chosen breeds and to attempt, by controlled breeding, to produce a dog which complied as nearly as possible to the standard. At the same time breeders attempted to preserve the qualities which had made the breed attractive and enabled it to carry out the tasks for which it had originally been used.

The interest in dogs created the need for breed societies and for dog shows, which in turn added impetus to the development of breeds. It is recorded that the first Rottweiler to be exhibited was at Heilbronn in 1882 and from its description it is obvious that it bore little resemblance to the present day Rottweiler. In 1899 the International Club for Leonbergers and Rottweiler Dogs was founded by Albert Kull. This rather unlikely pairing stemmed from the desire of its founder to stimulate interest in the two breeds originating from the German district of Swabia. This club did in fact publish in 1901 a breed standard based on one drawn up in 1883 by Hertneck and Kull. While its physical requirements, or breeders' interpretation of them, have changed to a considerable degree, the demands as to character still remain today. Little came of this first club and it was not until 1907 that two clubs catering exclusively for the Rottweiler were formed, the German Rottweiler Club (DRK) and South German Rottweiler Club (SDRK). The SDRK issued a standard which is of interest by virtue of its desire for a pincer bite, a requirement which will be discussed in detail in Chapter 12 on the Standard. The SDRK was short lived and soon merged into a third club, the International Rottweiler Club (IRK). Anyone familiar with the history of UK breed clubs, for virtually any breed, will not be surprised to hear that there was considerable dissension between these clubs, not only as a matter of inter-club rivalry, but also as to the details of the standard, coupled with disputes as to what should be the priorities for breeding. This particular argument boiled down to type versus character, an argument which is still with us today, although in our opinion they must be given equal weight. It is absurd to have a dog of good temperament which is totally untypical of a Rottweiler. It is equally absurd to have the opposite, a magnificent Rottweiler which is either uncontrollably nervous or aggressive.

A significant event for the Rottweiler was his official recognition in 1910 as a police dog. The other breeds recognized at this time were the GSD, Dobermann and Airedale. The hardworking old soldier had found himself a new role and a new future. His use as a police dog meant that breeders started to develop those aspects which made him suitable for such work. Obviously it became important to retain the basic courage, determination, power and tracking and biting ability which the breed already possessed. Selective breeding ingrained these characteristics even more deeply. Having said that, one finds that most of the early police Rottweilers came from those registered with the DRK and that these dogs differed considerably from our ideal today. Looking at pictures of two of the most famous of those early police Rottweilers, Rusz vom Bruckenbuckel and Max von der Strahlenburg, one sees lightly built dogs, hound-like, even bitchy heads, little stop, long narrow muzzle, large ears, long sloping croups and tucked up loins.

The IRK on the other hand concentrated on breeding a dog that would win in the show ring. In particular they looked for uniformity of appearance and refinement of the head. Their first great sire was Leo von Canstatt. In Leo's great-grandson Lord von der Teck we start to see a Rottweiler of the type we desire today. In particular Lord gave us the broad but dry head and shorter muzzle, coupled with an improved top and bottom line. He sired some sixty-three litters. Lord mated to his full sister Minna von der Teck produced Arco Torfwerk, sire of one hundred litters. From these dogs came a long line of great winners and they can be considered as the foundation stock of the modern Rottweiler. It is interesting to speculate, in view of the great success of the brother/sister mating of Lord and Minna, why the Germans set their face against what we call line-breeding: not perhaps as close as brother and sister, but certainly the classic grandfather, granddaughter mating. Would they have arrived at today's Rottweiler much earlier than they did and would the quite wide variation in type still to be found have disappeared?

At this stage it is of interest to look at the physical changes in the Rottweiler between the first standard and today. The ideal height and weight in 1883 were given as about 23.5 inches and 66 pounds. Actual measurements recorded during the First World War give heights around 21.5 inches for bitches and 24 inches for dogs. Weights are given as between 45 lbs to 57 lbs for bitches and 54 lbs to 61 lbs for dogs. We are, therefore, looking at dogs which were about a couple of inches lower at the shoulder than the present day Rottweiler, but only about half the weight which we expect today. In other words a much more leggy, lightly built dog, lacking the broad deep chest, strongly muscled hind-quarters and thick bone which we look for at present. Looking at photographs of top winning dogs in the early 1900s we see a long pointed muzzle, slight stop, heavy pendulous ears, relatively narrow chest, considerable tuck-up in the loins, straight in stifle and lacking angulation, long sloping croup with tail set low and carried down. By the 1920s we are looking at dogs with a well defined stop, shorter and broader muzzle, smaller and better placed ears, level top and bottom line, shorter, broader croup without excess slope and tail carried level with the back. Still in some cases a fairly leggy dog, but heavier boned and obviously weighing considerably more than earlier dogs. In the 1930s photographs show us a dog very similar to what we see today: a broad skull, dry head, ears still perhaps a little large but improving, slightly shorter in the leg, heavier boned and with the deep chest and level top and bottom line even more evident. The late 1950s produced the dog Harras vom Sofienbusch. Harras was the German *Bundessieger* for 1960, 1961 and 1962 and became an International and American Champion. At that time he probably represented the culmination of the sixty years of development we have been discussing, embodying all those desirable features which we admire today. At the time, in our opinion, he was outstanding among his contemporaries. Today, thanks to the example he gave us, there are probably a considerable number of dogs which could claim to be his equal.

There are some who claim that the trends which have shown over sixty years still continue and that the Rottweiler of the 1970s and onwards is even shorter in muzzle, with stop more pronounced, skull more domed, body even deeper and legs even shorter than those of the fifties and sixties: a dog which has become too heavy and one in which breed points are starting to be exaggerated. While we would agree that such dogs are to be found, we consider that these animals are not correct and would be incapable of carrying out the original function of the breed. However, we are firmly of the opinion that the majority of stock today does not fall into this category.

Credit for the steady development of the breed during the
first half of the twentieth century must go first of all to those
early pioneers and the original clubs, but the greatest praise
must go to their successors represented by the Allgemeiner
Deutscher Rottweiler Klub (ADRK). In August 1921 the
DRK and IRK combined to form the ADRK and an agreed
compromise standard was adopted. In 1923 it was agreed
that the only colour was to be black with tan markings. Other
colours were no longer accepted. In subsequent years long-
coated dogs were banned from breeding. White patches on
the chest almost disappeared. Emphasis was very much on
appearance and show qualities. Ear carriage improved. The
Rottweiler became squarer with greater clarity of outline.
While the process of refinement of the breed's show
qualities continued up to the early forties it would be a mistake to consider that those controlling the breed lost sight
of its working qualities. That they did not is shown by the
Rottweiler's continuing popularity as a police and army dog.
There is no doubt that those guiding the breed not only
improved its appearance but developed those aspects which
gave it its quality as a police dog. Its sheer power, coupled
with agility, courage and determination, ability to bite and
bite hard and its above-average tracking ability have always
ensured that the Rottweiler has an honoured place in the
ranks of working police dogs. The 1939–45 war did not limit
the breeding of Rottweilers in Germany to any great extent
and many were bred in German army kennels for work with
its armed forces. In 1943 four hundred and fifty were registered and in 1944 four hundred. By 1946 some eight
hundred were registered and these came from almost one
hundred different males and over one hundred females. By
1947 the annual total had reached thirteen hundred.

In 1943 the ADRK, ever watchful of the interests of the
breed, questioned whether the state of the breed truly
reflected the claim that 'the breeding of Rottweilers is the
breeding of working dogs'. As a result a number of new
regulations were introduced. Both parents must have been
passed as suitable for breeding. These requirements were
intended to ensure that they were both good specimens of
the breed without any major faults. In addition the regu-

lations required that a bitch might not have more than one litter per year and that the stud dog should not mate more than two bitches per week and not more than forty in any one year. Not more than six puppies were allowed to remain with the bitch and the use of a foster mother or artificial hand-rearing was forbidden unless the bitch became ill or died. In general these regulations continue to apply in Germany today, although the restriction on the number of puppies has been relaxed.

This chapter has been concerned with the origin and development of the breed in Germany. We have tried to show the changes which have taken place over some eighty years. During the last thirty years Rottweilers have also been actively bred in the UK, USA and elsewhere. It is interesting to note that despite the fiercely independent attitude of breeders in these countries the changes in the breed in Germany have been paralleled in the UK and USA. A comparison of photographs of British Rottweilers of the fifties and sixties with those of the seventies and eighties shows the same changes as have occurred in Germany. While it may be argued that British breeding has been based on imported German bloodlines, it is significant that both judges and breeders in both countries have chosen the same type at the same time. There is no doubt that, in the Rottweiler, Germany has given to the world an outstanding dog. The different national approaches to the breeding of dogs are discussed elsewhere. Suffice it to say that the Rottweiler, whose enormous explosion of popularity world wide during the seventies and eighties has been a virtually unique phenomenon, is the result of many years of dedicated and enlightened effort by the German breeders.

2

Character – Temperament and Ability

Writing on the origin of the Dobermann, Fred Curnow, one of Britain's greatest admirers of the breed, a man who did so much to put the Dobe in its present predominant position, said, 'The Rottweiler did much to bring the Dobe into being and those enthusiasts who work their dogs should deeply appreciate Louis Dobermann's foresight when deciding to introduce the blood of such an intelligent dog into his bloodlines.' Praise indeed from a man for whom the Dobermann was the world's greatest dog.

One of the few times that we found ourselves in disagreement with Fred Curnow was at the start of the Rottweiler's rise to fame when he said, 'you will have to Anglicize them.' We replied that if Anglicizing meant producing a male dog which could be shown on a thin show lead held by a couple of fingers, then we did not intend to do so. While admittedly it has brought its problems we preferred to see the breed retain those characteristics which made its reputation in Germany.

Whether you talk about character or temperament, and temperament seems to be the more favoured word, the behavioural characteristics of an animal weighing as much as many humans, and required to live in close proximity to them, must be of major importance. Many breed books deal with temperament in a few lines. Breed standards tend to give a brief idealistic outline and leave it at that. We consider that to have in-depth knowledge of the Rottweiler temperament, character and ability is essential before contemplating bringing one into your family and to enable you to enjoy your Rott to the full.

For this reason we are devoting a full chapter to the subject. The peasant farmers who developed the Rottweiler required a dog that would fulfil a wide range of needs. Not for them a number of highly specialized dogs, each for its own purpose. A peasant economy demands that each mouth needing to be fed must bear its share of tasks. Their ideal dog must be one that is big and courageous enough to guard the household, intelligent enough to be able to herd as well as guard cattle and other stock, and placid enough to lie on the hearth, be stepped over by the housewife and played with by the children. In addition the dog must be fast and agile enough to hunt in the forest and have the weight and strength to pull a small cart. Like his master, a Jack of all trades. A lot to find in one dog, and it is to the credit of those who developed the Rottweiler that they succeeded so well. Because for much of the breed's early life the Rottweiler carried out his duties in a relatively small area, these attributes were deeply ingrained in the breed and remain strong to this day.

As we said earlier all these characteristics are described in a slightly idealistic fashion in the General Appearance section of the Standard. What is not mentioned is that each of these characteristics creates a further derivative characteristic which must be appreciated if one is to understand the Rottweiler.

The best known characteristic of the Rottweiler must be his boldness and courage, to which we would add determination, confidence and the will to dominate. His certainty of his own superiority encourages him to tackle virtually anything. Rotts have been known to enter into battle with horses, bulls and motor cars. On each occasion they have won. At least one showed that he was perfectly willing to deal with an armoured car while another pair very quickly shredded a large man-carrying hot air balloon which landed in their exercising paddock. The fact that the balloon descended from the heavens giving off loud roaring noises was no deterrent at all. The Rottweiler, and in particular the male, is convinced that he is the greatest thing on four legs. Should anything or anybody suggest that he is not he is quite prepared to prove it. A meeting between two males produces the classic situation of an irresistible force meeting an immovable object. This confidence in his own superiority means, in the show ring, that while Rott breed classes tend to be taut with controlled aggression – at least one hopes that it is controlled – the solitary Rott in a class of mixed breeds, after a glance round to see that there is no foe worthy of his mettle, will treat all other breeds with calm disdain. It is possible to simplify the above by saying that the Rottweiler male is aggressive towards other dogs. This is true. However, you will better understand this character-istic if you realize that it is not just a wish to bite other dogs, but the natural reaction of a dominant male determined to retain his position of superiority. It is an accepted fact that males of any breed who are outstandingly successful as stud dogs tend to be aggressive towards other males. It does not need a dog expert to tell you that this is nature's way of keeping the strain strong.

Aggression, of course, is something that can be shown towards humans as well as dogs. While dog fights may be frightening and even dangerous, a Rottweiler deliberately attacking a human is totally unacceptable unless the dog is defending his owner or his owner's property or is a trained guard dog. In twenty-five years of owning Rottweilers and probably dealing with more of them than anyone else in this country, looking after them in boarding kennels, showing, training and whelping them, the writers have only been bit-ten twice. On each occasion it happened when trying to sort out a fight between two dogs and on each occasion the Rott has shown his sorrow when he realized that he had made a mistake. Basically the Rott is not aggressive towards humans; his natural instinct is to serve and love his owner. He does, however, demand that the relationship between dog and man is one of mutual respect. He is prepared to work with you and for you because he wishes to please you. He will not accept the situation where you attempt to make him obey you because he is too frightened to do anything else. Male Rotts are not easily frightened. The secret of suc-cess with a Rott is to ask him nicely. Attempts to dominate a Rott by brute force, or even by the verbal threat of force, will result in the dog reacting in the opposite direction to that in which you wish him to go. A fully grown male is not only as heavy as many humans but probably better muscled and certainly better co-ordinated. Only a strong and power-ful man would win a trial of physical strength with an adult male Rottweiler and even then it would be a painful process with very little achieved at the end of it.

The intelligence and courage of the Rottweiler have made him attractive to police forces and other organizations requiring a highly trained working dog. The instinct to defend his owner, his family and his property are inherent in the breed. Should the need arise he will defend you and yours with his life. It is a sad fact but one to remember with honour that many Rottweilers have done just that. You will find that under the circumstances of normal domestic life, your Rottweiler who lives as a friend and companion of the family will do all that is required of him without any encouragement to guard. Unless you need and are able to control a very tough guard dog, you should not attempt to encourage your dog in aggression against humans. If you do you will very soon have a dog that will be totally unsuitable to live the life of a normal domestic pet. Furthermore, do not be surprised if your Rottweiler does not start to guard until about eighteen months or two years of age. The young dog has the natural pack instinct to 'leave it to father' and he may very well be content to sit back and leave you or an older dog to do the guard work until he is sure of his place in the hierarchy. One young dog of ours lived with his father and an older bitch until he was fifteen months of age. When the bitch told him off for misbehaviour he would go and sit behind father. So much so that we decided that the dog was too soft to be typical. However, when he went to his new owner he immediately accepted responsibility for his new home and family and very quickly acquired a reputation as a tough and determined guard, although gentle and loving with his owners.

The Rott's determination to dominate means that if he is to accept you as his pack leader then you must be an even stronger character than he is. By strength we are not talking about physical strength but the confidence in yourself which in the Rott gives him his ability to remain in command. Not infrequently owners have failed to establish a successful relationship with their dog because deep down inside they are frightened of him. Equally if an owner is too polite, too retiring by nature, or if he believes that one should not show anger, merely reasoned persuasion, then the Rott will very quickly decide that if no one else is going to be boss, then he will. It must never enter your mind that the dog is either going to attack you or refuse to obey you. If it does then the dog will know and you will have started to lose the battle. If a Rottweiler does show resentment at what he is being asked to do then the answer is to ignore it, at the same time firmly but calmly ensuring that he does what you wish. In our opinion, although some trainers will not agree, bribery is perfectly acceptable in such circumstances and often helps to solve a problem.

On a few occasions our own Rotts have chosen to defy us. On each occasion, rather than pursue the situation to an actual physical confrontation, we have relaxed, called the dog to us in a friendly manner, the dog has come forward tail wagging, nuzzled our hand and received a word of encouragement and a pat in return. Honour was satisfied on both sides. Domination by the human without loss of face to dog or man. No one had backed down, no one had won. The ultimate aim of mutual respect in the Man–Rottweiler relationship had been achieved.

While 'placid' well describes a Rottweiler at rest, he is perhaps better described as having the calm self-assurance of a strong man who knows that he can cope with any problem. Stemming from the conviction of his ability to handle any situation comes a characteristic which we have never found so well developed in any other breed: the ability to decide whether what is happening around him needs his attention as a guard or his gentleness as a friend. In incident after incident we have found that the Rottweiler is able to differentiate between these needs. He is able to decide from the inflection in his owner's voice whether his master is alarmed by what is happening or not. He has the ability to differentiate between the butcher and the burglar. The owner's friendly 'good morning' to a man never seen before who is delivering a parcel will create no guarding reaction, but a slight edge in one's voice as one repeats to the over-persistent caller that his services are not required is enough to make your dog alert and protective.

Now let us look at the Rottweiler's intelligence. One look at that broad skull should tell you that there is plenty of room for brains. Intelligent he certainly is. Biddable is a word which well describes his keen brain combined with his desire to please. Because he is intelligent it follows that he has the ability to think. Not for the Rottweiler that mechanical obedience which one finds in some breeds. He is not a dog who will repeatedly and slavishly obey what to him seem pointless orders. Teach a Rottweiler to jump a 3-foot jump and the first time he is ordered to jump he will do it perfectly, the second time he will do it, and the third time he is likely to sit on one side or the other and if he could speak would say, 'make your mind up, which side do you want me?' While some trainers will say that this is laziness we prefer to believe that it is intelligence.

The Rott has a great deal of mental ability. You will find that from a very early age he is able to absorb simple training and will soon begin to think for himself. This brain power needs to be channelled in the direction in which you, his owner, desire. Failure to train this intelligent breed in at least elementary obedience will result in his using his intelligence purely for his own ends. Furthermore, you will lose much of the pleasure of ownership if you do not create that bond between dog and man, and also the pride in your own achievement, that a well-trained dog can bring.

For various reasons people tend to categorize dogs. The Kennel Club division into various groups – working, gundog, hound, utility, etc. – has the effect of escalating this trend. The very reasonable suggestion that the Working Group, which includes the Rottweiler, should be split into, say, Pastoral, i.e. Herding and Guard groups, would immediately cause a problem as to which group the Rottweiler should go into. Much of the breed's reputation has been built on his ability as a guard. However, one should not lose sight of the fact that Rottweilers were originally used as herding dogs, in particular for cattle, and the instinct and ability are still there. There are many modern instances of Rottweilers working successfully as herding dogs on farms both in Britain and abroad. Apart from the obvious job of herding cattle, they have worked sheep not only in this country but as far afield as Australia. Many owners will tell you of the Rott's natural herding ability showing in their dog's liking for rounding up the domestic ducks and chickens.

The Rottweiler's ability to use his nose for scenting purposes must, we would think, rate him in the top ten or even higher in suitability for nose work, either in tracking or searching. Certainly in police forces who in general favour the GSD for their work, a really difficult track or search usually results in a call to 'bring out the Rottweiler' if one is available. Rottweilers are used for rescue work in Europe, searching forests and snow-covered ground for missing persons. While in working trials the Rott may not be as fast or agile as some other breeds, his tracking ability almost invariably enables him to do well.

The Germans rate the Rottweiler's 'searching instinct' as medium. They also consider that he does not have a well-developed hunting instinct. Certainly, unlike some breeds we could name, he does not put his nose down to the trail of a rabbit and disappear, deaf to all recall orders, over the nearest horizon. At the same time a trained Rottweiler will do an area search with great thoroughness while the untrained one will search his territory with enthusiasm, running down any interesting scents. Our own Champion Chesara Dark Charles prides himself as a rabbit-hunter and occasionally comes trotting back from the paddock proudly carrying his catch. Champion Chesara Akilles preferred pheasants which he would stalk until they took off and then catch in flight about two feet above the ground. Many of our Rotts would retrieve both fur and feather and the interesting point is that all of them would deliver their catch to hand without mouthing or damage. Portlaynum Bridgitte once walked around for several minutes with mouth tightly closed and looking pleased with herself. When she was forced to open her mouth, a wren literally flew from her jaws. Although it would be absurd to say that the Rottweiler has claims as a gundog, several are so used, and in spite of their ability to bite very hard the breed is actually quite soft-mouthed.

Away from the stimulus of other males or the need to guard, a Rottweiler may well be described as placid. Asleep on his own hearthrug, surrounded by his family, he will take life very calmly. The question so often asked, and it is of obvious importance, is, are Rottweilers good with children? Of course the immediate answer is, are your children good with dogs? If you own the sort of child who, when shown a puppy, immediately starts to find out whether the legs unscrew, then we suggest that you either get rid of the child or deny yourself the pleasure of owning a Rottweiler! With this sort of child the puppy will first of all suffer, and it may even be injured. In the long run it will remember and resent such treatment. When fully grown, or even half grown, a Rott is a powerful animal, and even a warning snap telling the child not to do that again could cause serious injury. That said, and given proper upbringing on both sides, many a child has been brought up with a Rottweiler as its constant companion and guard and has been safe in this modern world by having a 'dark guardian of the family' close at its side. We know of one breeder whose youngest addition to the family – and additions occur quite frequently – is usually to be found curled up in the dog bed with the family Rottweiler bitch. This even applies when the bitch has a litter. She seems to accept without question this cuckoo in the nest. So Rottweilers *are* good with children. However, remember that even a nine-month old puppy is big, bois-terous and bouncy. He can easily knock over a young child. It is also important to remember that a baby rolling on the ground and perhaps screaming does not necessarily rep-resent to a Rottweiler a young human. The scream and apparent helplessness can give the impression of an injured creature. The basic instinct of a dog, any dog, is to attack such a creature. At the very least the dog may decide that this is a toy to be treated in the same way as his old shoe and favourite bone. You would be very foolish to leave a dog alone with a young child until you are satisfied that the dog fully understands that his duty is to guard and treasure the child. Give him time and understanding and the Rott will do just this.

Continuing our study of the mental characteristics which, combined with his physical description, make the Rottweiler the dog he is, what are the effects of his weight, strength, speed of movement and agility? The Rottweiler was used extensively in Europe as a working draught dog. Let a Rott pull on his lead and you will soon learn that he has not lost the ability to lean into a load. Before you decide that a super-market trolley pulled by a Rottweiler is the answer to bringing home the groceries, we must remind you that it is illegal in the UK to use a dog to pull a cart on the public highway. An 1890 photograph of a Rottweiler harnessed to quite a substantial cart laden with boxes and barrels shows his woman handler harnessed alongside him and bending her back to the load. Modern photographs usually show a rather large lady seated in an elaborate cart, the whole outfit dwarfing the dog, rather like the travel photographs of a Chinese coolie pulling his rickshaw laden with a large European. Suffice it to say at this stage that, like his other inherited virtues, the Rott has not lost his ability as a draught dog.

Speed and agility must, in the Rottweiler, be related to his overall build, size and weight. In the same way that one cannot criticize the lack of running or jumping ability in a heavyweight boxer, it would be equally absurd, as some working trials enthusiasts do, to make invidious comparisons between the Rottweiler and, say, a Border Collie. The two breeds have been developed for different purposes and you must remember the wide variety of tasks that the Rottweiler can undertake. Bearing in mind that one of his original functions was probably the hunting of wild boar, he had to be fast enough to catch his quarry and heavy enough to hold it when he did. For all his size the Rott can produce a remarkable turn of speed over a short distance. Equally at a steady trot he can cover long distances as he had to when driving cattle. His short back and powerful muscles allow him to turn quickly and, as anyone who has walked up behind a Rott who happens to be looking the other way will find out, the dog can turn on the spot at remarkable speed so that you suddenly find that his teeth are where his tail was a second before. In agility competitions, while lacking the sinuous sleekness of some breeds, the Rott performs his exercises with a combination of enthusiasm, fearlessness and accuracy. He has the ability to jump with reasonable ease. The standard 3-foot clear jump used in Working Trials presents no problem to a Rottweiler. Many of them of their own volition will jump much higher obstacles. The scale or climb over a vertical wall is not an exercise which we like to see a Rottweiler perform. The UK Working Trial requirement is for a 6-foot vertical wooden wall. To see a Rottweiler tackle this obstacle is to see a courageous, determined dog straining his heart out to succeed. He will jump at the top, get a grip with his forelegs and then struggle and heave to get the rest of himself over the top. Having got over the top he is then faced with getting down the other side, usually by dropping, although some will try to scramble down. Either way he tends to put his full weight on landing on his fore end with the very real risk of injury. In our opinion the 6-foot scale should be replaced by the 'A' frame giving an inclined slope both going up and coming down. As we said, the Rott shows his courage on the scale, but no trainer should demand such effort from a dog built the way a Rottweiler is.

The memory of the Rottweiler is worthy of discussion. Vets and others complain that after undergoing treatment with the owner holding and controlling the dog, during which time he has been perfectly behaved, the Rott will, some minutes later when everyone has relaxed, attack the vet. This is usually described as unprovoked aggression. We prefer to believe that in the Rott's mind he had adequate provocation during the treatment but was prepared to forego his objection as long as his owner was telling him to behave. However, once it was over the dog saw no reason to refrain from expressing his annoyance.

Certainly Rotts have long memories. It is not unusual for a puppy who left his breeder at eight weeks of age to show obvious signs of recognition if brought back to his birthplace at twelve months or more. Often his new owner comments that he does not normally take kindly to strangers but it is very apparent that to the Rott his breeder is not a stranger. Obedience training, once learnt by a Rott, will remain with him for the rest of his life even though it may not be practised for years. Equally if he takes a dislike to a person this aversion will remain and surface when the dis-liked person appears even though there may be long gaps in between.

Some writers have described the Rottweiler as stubborn. If stubbornness is another word for determination then you could describe him as stubborn. However, if you accept the more usual meaning of the word to imply awkwardness, cussedness, unwillingness to obey or even stupidity, then 'stubborn' does not in any way describe his character. In our experience the Rottweiler is extremely biddable, anxious to please without being servile and likes nothing better than to earn his master's praise.

We have gone into the subject of the Rottweiler's character and ability in considerable depth. As we said at the beginning of this chapter, we consider it essential to do so.

3

The Rottweiler in Great Britain

Writing in 1982, Stanley Dangerfield, who has long cast a penetrating eye over the British dog scene, defined the British dog breeder in terms which we have always treasured and remembered. He said, 'Good breeders, be it of dogs, horses, sheep or even white mice, are individualists. Loners. Dyed in the wool self-employed persons . . . and as often as not, eccentric into the bargain. Not for them adherence to the word from above. They do their own thing even if it means defying authority, losing favour, resigning or even cheating. They believe they know more than "big brother" about their own specialized subject and as often as not they do. Even if not, their platform is, "These are my animals, it's my house and it's my money. Others can suggest, but nobody can tell me what to do." Herein lies the secret of British breeders. They are independent, stubborn, self-opinionated and frequently eccentric to the point of being slightly potty.'

Contained in those words of Stanley Dangerfield's are all the answers to those in Britain who clamour for the German system of control through breed clubs and breed wardens. Can you think of one person who would be acceptable to you as the Chief Breed Warden? Even more unlikely, can you think of anyone in your general area you would accept as your Area Breed Warden? During a very pleasant weekend with Dr Wilfried Peiper, President of the German Kennel Club (VDH), we discussed our two countries' approach to dog breeding. We agreed that we started at diametrically opposed positions. The German approach is firm control with clearly laid down regulations aimed at preventing any person from harming the breed. Our own approach allows anyone to 'do their own thing' with the only

restraint being the judges' opinion, the willingness of the
public to buy stock and to a lesser degree the pressure of
public opinion as to what is, or is not, ethical. What we did
agree on was that when we met in the centre, in the show
ring, one saw dogs of the same quality. In other words both
systems worked equally well as far as the excellence of the
dogs was concerned. In all probability what both countries
have is the system which suits them best. The argument
often put forward that the German system of control would
obviate mass breeding for profit, the activities of the puppy
farmer and the foisting on the pet-buying public of poor
quality stock at high prices is not true. It is still possible to
breed dogs in Germany outside the breed control system.
What such breeders cannot provide are the registration and
pedigree documents which to many pet owners are
unimportant.

As a percentage of its total population Britain probably
has more dog enthusiasts – that is, people who breed, show,
judge or train dogs – than any other country in the world.
The old joke that there is a dog expert on every street corner
came true for the early Rottweiler owner who, taking his
dog for a walk, would find himself constantly asked what
breed his dog was, or very frequently being told what combination of other breeds had gone into its creation. The
Rottweiler as a breed was totally unknown to the British
world of dogs as late as the early sixties. At this time a
famous all-rounder judge knowledgeable about hundreds of
breeds, doing the commentary at a major championship
show, let slip, 'It's a what?' when told that the dog entering
the ring was a Rottweiler. Major dog books published at this
time made no mention of the breed or dismissed it in a
few lines.

The first recorded importation of Rottweilers into Britain
was in 1936 by the late Mrs Thelma Gray. Already famous
for her Alsatians and Corgis under the Rozavel prefix, she
brought in two adult bitches from Germany, one of them in
whelp. Unfortunately only one of this litter survived. Subsequent imports by Thelma Gray and others totalled five,
including the bitch Int. Ch. Vefa v. Kohlerwald, again mated
before entering the country. The whole litter died in
quarantine. Although Thelma Gray attempted to safeguard
her Rotts during the war years by shipping most of them to

Eire, they disappeared without trace. Certainly the odd Rottweiler was still in Britain during the 1939–45 war. We have included a photograph of one taken about 1941, but regrettably have no details of its breeding or what happened to it. Through the kindness of Mrs Daphne Cargen we do know that it was called Jan and that it was about two years old in 1941. The owner was a Mrs Holland of Marlborough, Wilts. One further record exists: a coloured cigarette card in a series on breeds of dogs. This card, which is an artist's impression, is obviously taken from a photograph of one of Thelma Gray's dogs. As the photo was in black and white the artist had no idea of the actual colour of the dog, so he coloured it a nice chocolate brown!

One can only wonder what the history of Rottweilers in Britain would have been if the war had not intervened. It is quite certain that in the hands of experienced breeders of the calibre of Thelma Gray, coupled with the fact that the stock she imported was of high quality – one was an International Champion – the breed would have got off to a better start than it did fifteen years later. For all practical purposes the pre-war Rottweilers vanished without trace and play no part in the post-war history.

The story of British Rottweilers starts not in Britain but in Germany after the war, when a number of dog-minded servicemen saw the breed and were impressed. Our own first contact was in 1949 while trying to sort out a minor frontier incident, when, as was said at the time, 'the only person on either side who was not in a "flap" was the East German Police Rottweiler,' who stood four square in the middle of the road ready to sort out the whole problem in his own way the moment his handler gave the word. Once seen never forgotten, and occasionally one would see these big, black, powerful dogs walking at the side of their masters. However, all dogs were rare in Germany in those days and pedigree stock were usually kept out of sight. Too many of the top dogs had already gone overseas in the hands of British or US servicemen, in circumstances which did not bear too close examination. We bought a Boxer in 1950 and the transaction was conducted in a lonely farmhouse at dead of night after a chain of contacts which would have done credit to a spy thriller.

The first person to put his admiration of the Rottweiler

into practical effect was an Army Veterinary Surgeon, Capt Roy-Smith, who on leaving Germany imported a pair, Ajax v. Fuhrenkamp and Berny v. Weyher. We are not being unfair to Capt Roy-Smith if we say that neither of these were outstanding specimens. As we have said, it was almost impossible to buy good quality stock in Germany in those days. What is important is that he made a start. The bitch, Berny, was heavy, if not long coated, and the dog, Ajax, left much to be desired. Nothing came of the first pair but Roy-Smith then brought in a second bitch, Lotte v. Oesterburg, who had a litter to Ajax. Little was to come of their matings, with this one notable exception. In 1958 they produced Rintelna the Bombardier, of whom more later. As will be seen, the Bombardier formed one half of the foundation stock in the UK.

In 1954 and 1955 Mrs Joanna Chadwick imported Rudi Eulenspiegel and Quinta Eulenspiegel. The Eulenspiegel prefix owned by Frl Marianne Bruns had been well known in Germany for many years. This pair can be said to be the other half of the original foundation stock. As a foundation these two halves probably reflected the state of the breed at that time. The two strains showed great variation in size and conformation. While Roy-Smith's imports were relatively light animals, the Eulenspiegels tended to be massive in size. Under Joanna Chadwick's prefix of Mallion, Rudi and Quinta produced a number of litters from which came several dogs which helped to establish the fame of the breed. Two – Abelard and Brutus – went to the Metropolitan Police and established reputations as hard, tough dogs, very successful in their work. In 1957 a dog was born which did much to popularize Rottweilers, not so much from the show side but as a character and a working dog. This was Bruin of Mallion, usually known as 'Copper' and owned by Mrs Maud Wait. Copper was a big powerful dog and in the hands of Maud Wait, a superb trainer, he became the first Rottweiler Working Trials Champion qualifying CD, UD ex., TD ex. The combination of Maud and Copper certainly gave the breed a lot of welcome publicity. Our own first introduction to Rottweilers in Britain was when we met Maud in a hotel where she was staying with Copper and Lenlee Neeruam Brigitte CD ex, UD ex. We sat in the hotel lounge with Maud

and her two dogs all evening talking about Rotts. About
11.30 p.m. we said, 'Maud, the only thing we have not heard
is your dogs barking.' Maud gave the command 'speak' and
that magnificent Rottweiler bellow echoed down the cor-
ridors. Doors flew open, the Manager appeared and soon
after we departed, utterly smitten with Rotts. Brigitte was
mated to Copper and produced a second Rottweiler Working Trials Champion, Lenlee Gladiaor CD ex, UD ex, TD ex,
PD ex.

In the late fifties and early sixties far more attention was
being paid to the Rottweiler's working ability than to his
show potential. In obedience and even more in working
trials, the Rott's brain and trainability gave him a reputation
and success-rate far in excess of his numerical strength.
Mary Macphail by now owned Rintelna the Bombardier and
qualified him CD ex, UD ex. In the North the Garlands
worked Brunnhilde of Mallion in obedience with success.
Sgt Blundy, a serving police officer, achieved CD ex with
Argolis Ettare, bred by Joan Wheatcroft.

All this emphasis on the working qualities of the
Rottweiler brought the breed to the attention of the public
in a way which showed off its best qualities. Teams of
Rottweilers gave displays of obedience and working ability
at shows and village fêtes. Jumping ahead to the sixties a
team of Rottweilers gave a half-hour demonstration every
night for ten days at the Schoolboys' and Schoolgirls'
Exhibition held at Olympia in London. This included the
retrieve of an egg by Manzai Kala Koota CD ex, UD ex, PD ex,
TD owned by Ivor Fisher. After the retrieve of the egg Ivor
used to break it to prove that it was real and uncooked. The
finale of this display was when the children were invited to
come and pat the dogs. Rottweilers who a few minutes
before had been doing man work would disappear under a
swarm of children, the only visible part being a wagging tail.
Both Rotts and owners had a lot of fun in those days.

By 1960 it is probable that there were less than one
hundred Rottweilers in this country, many of them in pet
homes. However, the breed had begun to catch the eye of a
small group of enthusiasts while still being virtually
unknown to the general world of dogs.

In the show world, taking Crufts as a yardstick, 1958 saw

seven Rottweilers entered. By 1962 this had risen to sixteen.
Even by 1967, the second year that C.C.s were on offer for
the breed, the entry was still only sixteen rising to twenty-
six in 1968.

By the early sixties the breed was in the hands of a very
small group of breeders working hard to get it established.
To a certain extent the breed had become a cult. Many
owners argued that it was not as other dogs. That its
intelligence, strength and strong guarding instinct made it a
specialist dog only to be owned by those with an understanding of its nature. Some, admittedly with some justification,
feared the effects of popularity on the breed and had no wish
to encourage ownership by the general dog-owning public.
Regrettably, events during the last twenty-five years have
proved that there were good grounds for such apprehen-
sions. The failure has not been in the Rottweiler, who has
remained the dog he always was, but in his misuse by
humans, the failure by owners to understand the type of dog
he is and in the activities of 'breeders' whose sole interest in
the breed has been as a means of making money.

The hard fact was that the breeding base was too limited.
By 1964 every Rottweiler in this country, and there were
several hundred of them, stemmed from eight imported
animals; nine if you count one that did not come in but sent
his bloodlines over in an in-whelp bitch. Of these, several
produced very little, narrowing the field still more.

The Rottweiler male of the period tended to be a heavily
built animal with a very strong head, carrying fairly
excessive wrinkle. Entropion was far too common a condition which was aggravated by the Standard's demand for
an almond eye being interpreted as a small eye buried in
wrinkle.

One strain tended to large over-rounded heads, a type
which would be described as 'apple-headed' in some breeds.
Ears were often over-large and set too low. Backs were apt to
be longer than desirable. Movement, as ever in the big
breeds, was a problem. Bitches were inclined to be the
opposite to dogs in many ways. Bitch heads were frequently
narrow in skull and muzzle. Many bitches were small, light-
boned animals, although at the same time other bitches
were large, long in back and hound-like in head.

This assessment of the Rottweiler at this period does not in any way detract from the progress that had been made, but it was obvious that the interest of the general public in the breed had to be increased, if only to ensure a reasonable market for stock that would allow breeders to plan breeding programmes for improvement.

To those of us who wished to see the breed prosper, and by now there was a growing number of dedicated and knowledgeable enthusiasts, it was obvious that the prime need was to import sires who could upgrade the overall quality, and that such dogs be chosen and used in a deliberate and planned programme. Up to this time sheer lack of numbers had meant that matings took place purely on a 'what is available' basis, rather than the careful mating of dog to bitch to achieve definite aims.

The Rottweiler Club was formed in 1960 by Maud Wait who became its first Secretary. You could also say that for the early years it was Maud's enthusiasm and energy, supported by a few others, which provided most of the impetus. The Chairman was Capt Roy-Smith MRCVS and Mary Macphail was Treasurer. From now on the breed had a body actively working for its interests. The club's list of officers and committee for 1963 shows that a few of those early enthusiasts are still active in the breed at the time of writing. Apart from Mary Macphail and ourselves, Reg Kelly from Northern Ireland is still involved, Joan Wheatcroft still takes a keen interest and is always a welcome visitor at shows for her fund of anecdotes of the early days, while Betty Bensley, now Baxter, although no longer active in Rotts, is still very much involved in the dog scene. Rottweilers in Britain owe much to that small band whose love for a breed that few people had even heard of, and even fewer had seen, laid the foundations for the future.

By 1965 the breed had begun to be firmly established in Britain. Registrations were running at about 150 per year. The next stage was to persuade the Kennel Club to grant the breed a separate register. Under the regulations a separate register meant that Challenge Certificates would be on offer for the breed. The first requirement for a separate register was an official Kennel Club Standard. This was produced by a committee of which the writers and Mary Macphail are the

only members still involved. We were lucky to have Thelma
Gray as a member, able to give us the benefit of her years of
experience. We set ourselves guidelines in that our aim was
to reproduce in English the then current German Standard.
The only amendments we wished to make were where the
German Standard contravened the general requirements of
the Kennel Club. We were also most anxious to capture the
'spirit' of the original German while at the same time ensuring that we did not fall into error by a too literal translation.
Our criterion was to ensure that nothing was written into
the Standard which would lead to an unsound animal or anything described as desirable which, if exaggerated, could act
to the dog's detriment. Each word was weighed, defined and
argued about. Some of the discussion got very involved. As
an example of how easy it is to go astray, an eminent lady, no
longer in the breed, argued that movement should include
the demand for single tracking, what has been called the
'string of pearls'. That is, if the dog's footprints were embed-
ded in, say, snow, the resultant pattern would be a single line
of paw prints. The argument was supported by a claim that
the Germans also required this although nothing appeared
in the Standard. We tracked this down and found that the
lady in question had, in the past, owned a dog which single
tracked. She wrote to Germany asking about this type of
movement and received the polite reply that this type of
movement was also known in Germany. That was interpreted as being a statement that the Germans thought this
type of movement to be desirable. While everyone agreed
that a dog's feet do in fact move in towards the centre line
when moving, we were able to persuade the lady concerned
that such a requirement would lead to an unsound dog. So
the Rottweiler did not move into the future with single
tracking being listed as desirable.

Eventually we decided that we had got it right. Before
taking it to the Kennel Club we asked a number of very
senior veterinary surgeons to examine the draft to ensure
that it contained no requirements which could be harmful
to the dog. The vets gave it a clean bill of health and the next
stage was to achieve Kennel Club approval. This again
caused problems. The use of the words Zygomatic Arch was
queried and although it stayed in, the 1986 Standard has in

fact removed the term as being too technical. At last we had an official British Standard. No longer did judges have to be given a translation from the German or the American version. For those who believe that breed standards are handed down from on high, carved on tablets of stone, we can assure you that you are wrong. They are produced in smoke-filled rooms, by arguing people around a table, using their knowledge and love of the breed.

The next stage was the actual granting of C.C.s. The requirements were for at least three hundred dogs to be registered in a period of three years with at least one hundred and fifty registered in the last year. This involved a certain amount of sliding the registration figures up and down the time scale; the year did not have to start on 1 January. A large litter was pushed through quickly and we had our four sets of C.C.s starting with Crufts 1966. The other three shows which were allocated C.C.s were Birmingham National, the SKC, then at Kelvin Hall, Glasgow, and Paignton. Despite now having C.C.s we were still benched in some odd draughty, cobwebby corner, under the stairs, or up in the gallery. Entries, as we have said, were still very small. If you took long over your coffee break you not only missed your class, but the judging of the entire breed.

Back to the dogs themselves. We have already mentioned Argolis Ettare owned by Sgt Blundy. Mated to Rudi Eulenspiegel she produced in her first litter Portlaynum Bridgitte, born January 1962: Ronda, as we called her. We had been waiting with great impatience for our first Rottweiler. When the telephone call came to say that we could have her we arranged to pick her up in Boston in Lincolnshire. She was then four months old and our first sight of her was two thick-boned front legs ending in large feet draped over the back of the front seat of Blundy's car. We took one look, said, 'She'll do,' and she came to Chesara. Ronda was a great character: by today's standards a large, powerful bitch with a lot of determination. She soon established her place in our kennel of Boxers and Sussex Spaniels. There was only one place for Ronda – on top! She remained boss of all the kennel, including males, for the whole of her life. When the time came for her to be mated

we took a long look at the available stud dogs and decided on
Mary Macphail's Rintelna the Bombardier. Ronda had been
winning well in the show ring and was the first bitch to consistently break the male monopoly of Best of Breed. To us
the decision as to her mate was a vital one; it was our first
step towards the future, and events proved us right. From
this mating came Ch. Chesara Dark Destiny, the first
Rottweiler Show Champion in Britain. She did it in three
consecutive shows: SKC, Paignton and Birmingham National.
1966 therefore gave the breed not only championship status
but its first champion.

The Bombardier went on to sire two further champions in
one litter when mated to Anouk from Blackforest, a
daughter of the imported bitch Vera v. Filstalstrand: Horst
from Blackforest CD ex and Elizabeth Harrap's Hildegard
from Blackforest. He also sired Joan Woodgate's (now
Blackmore) Emil from Blackforest who as 'Panzer' achieved
fame as a dog star of film and TV, including a full length TV
film devoted almost entirely to himself called *Death of a
Rebel*.

As we have said, the time had come to import a sire who
could exert a major influence on the breed. This is easy to
say but not so easy to achieve. In the spring of 1964 we spent
a weekend touring kennels all over Holland. We looked at
puppies, we looked at their sires and dams and nothing
really pleased us. With us was the then Chairman of the
Netherlands Rottweiler Club, Mrs Teneke Boltjes, whose
kindness and help had made the visit possible. All the time in
the car we had with us her dog Ch. Baldur v. Habennichts.
We thought that he was wonderful both in type and temperament. It was getting towards the end of our visit and we
had not yet found what we wanted. 'Isn't there a litter by
Baldur?' we asked. 'There is,' she answered, 'but I didn't like
to appear to be pushing my own stock.' Late on a cold
gloomy afternoon we arrived at an isolated Dutch farm. We
were met at the gate by Astrida, mother of the litter, who
first guarded and then, after a word from her owner, greeted
us and led us proudly to see her litter. So we found
Champion Chesara Luther who became the second British
Rottweiler champion and the first male champion. He
gained his second C.C. at Birmingham National on the same

day that Destiny gained her title. Luther sired four champions, Chesara Dark Soliloquy, Chesara Dark Inquisitor, Portia Moriconium and Chesara Dark Opal. Luther was not everything that we desired. A big dog, he tended to be a little leggy with a very pleasing head and expression. Although he had good ear placement himself, he tended to throw rather large hound-like ears when mated to bitches of the lines already here.

Also in 1964 Mary Macphail imported from the USA Blackforest Rodsdens Jett v. Sofienbusch, sired by Harras v. Sofienbusch. Harras, whom we have already mentioned as probably representing the zenith of German breeding in the late fifties, was exported to the States in 1964. At the time of his importation by the Rodsdens kennels he was some six and a half years old. It was a tragedy for Mary and for the breed that for a number of reasons this son of Harras had no significant effect on Rottweilers in this country. In fact Harras did not contribute to British bloodlines other than in two great-grandsons: Peter and Joyce Radley's Ch. Castor of Intisari, imported in 1971 from Denmark, and Joan Woodgate's German import, Lars v.d. Hobertsberg, who came in in 1969. Castor twice produced two champions in one litter: Champions Adoram Cordelia and Adoram Lennart of Intisari, and Jagen Dust My Blues and Jagen Mr Blue. Lars died at the age of two, a great loss to the breed. Apart from siring Ch. Jentris Gerontius, his main gift to the breed was his outstanding soundness, a large percentage of his progeny receiving H. D. certificates. As we have seen, Harras bloodlines only came into Britain in a very diluted form. Neither was it possible to line-breed back to him as British breeders would have done if the stock had been available. In the mid-sixties we were offered a son of Harras. The dog was excellent but he was Sch. H3, the highest working qualification which included attack-work and we decided that while he would have caused a sensation with breeders and judges in Britain, it was likely that it would have been the type of sensation we did not require.

In 1966 we decided to import again. This time we had more definite ideas as to what we wanted. Luther, plus the stock that was already here, had, in our opinion, moved the breed in the right direction. This time we went to Sweden, to

Mrs Gerd Hyden. We gave her a list of the faults that the breed had and the particular points which we wished to improve. Filling our shopping list to our complete satisfaction she sent us Chesara Akilles by Int. and Nordic Champion Fandangos Fair Boy out of Dackes Ina: of medium size, short strong back, good top line, short croup with correct tail set, neat well-placed ears, dry head of the correct proportions and with a very appealing expression. As a character he was the ideal: courageous, tough and determined but a wonderful friend and companion. He was also a clown with a great sense of humour. Akilles sired ten champions. He did all that we had hoped, playing a major part in bringing the breed to the standard it has reached today. Such was his influence on the breed that breeders still try and breed as close back to him as possible, and in an apparent attempt to gain benefit from his fame his name has been used as a prefix.

Mrs Elsie Henbest used Akilles on Byxfield Anouk of Cenlea, a Ch. Horst of Blackforest daughter. One of this litter, Ch. Chesara Byxfield Akela, mated to an Akilles son, Ch. Chesara Dark Kruger, produced Chesara Dark Laura. Laura therefore carried two lines to Akilles. Laura was mated to a Dutch import, Joris. This dog came in as a family pet with his owner who was working in London. We saw Joris in quarantine, liked him and obtained his owner's permission to use him. To our knowledge he was only used twice before returning to Holland. He was a dog who moved superlatively and could have played a major part if he had remained in Britain. From the Laura/Joris mating came Ch. Chesara Dark Julia whose daughter Juliette, when put to Chesara Dark Herod, gave us Ch. Chesara Dark Charles. Used on Mrs Pat Lanz's Chesara Dark Intuition, Akilles sired Ch. Borgvaale Bonita, the dam of Mrs Rita Parratt's Ch. Borgvaale Lion City River of Ritonshay, another very successful sire. Bonita's duaghter, Borgvaale Venus, was the dam of Ch. Chesara Dark Roisterer, father of Juliette, thus creating another line back to Akilles.

We are aware that tracing these relationships through a number of generations can become confusing. However, this example illustrates the principles on which we have worked, which can be summarized as: using the best dogs available, ensuring that the male and female do not have similar faults and then line-breeding.

In 1967, Jim Baldwin, whose interest and ability in breeding show stock goes back a very long way and embraces not only dogs but birds, in both of which he has had considerable success, imported Ero v. Bucheneck. Ero, sired by the 1966 and 1967 *Bundessieger*, Emir v. Freienhagen, became a champion himself and sired two champions, Ch. Bhaluk Princess Birgitta to Elsa from Blackforest, and our own Ch. Chesara Dark Warlord. Joan Woodgate, as she then was, brought in Gamegards Bulli v. d. Waldachquelle. He sired a total of six champions including Ch. Schutz from Gamegards, a bitch we much admired, and Ch. Janbicca the Superman, owned and bred by Mrs Jane Bloom, and winner of fourteen C. C. s. Superman, on his dam's side, went back in three generations to Ch. Ero v. Bucheneck and Working Trials Champion Bruin of Mallion who was in at the beginning.

The sixties showed the breed making steady progress. While many names have been omitted the same sires and bloodlines repeatedly occur. There were many others who played a valuable part. The following decade saw the descendants of these imports start to play their part, with a steady flow of British bred dogs achieving honours in the ring.

In 1972 we went to Holland to attend a conference of the International Friends of Rottweilers (IFR), which was an attempt to bring together Rottweiler owners from all over the world. Although a number of such conferences have been held – the first was in Germany – they have not really given any great benefit, largely because of different approaches to breed control. However, at the second conference held in Holland we saw once again a bitch whom we thought was superb. Owned and bred by Leneke Gruter she became Int. and Ned. Ch. Facha Triomfator, the most beautiful bitch we had seen. We had first seen her as a young bitch on one of our previous visits and now she was fulfilling her promise. She had qualified Sch.H1 and we had been given a demonstration of her working ability at her owner's kennels. She had been shown in Germany on the Rottweilers' home ground and had won, attaining her international title. From the moment we first saw her we wanted one of her puppies. It was quite a long wait. No sire was good enough for such a beauty. The Dutch were carrying out extensive research into hip dysplasia at Utrecht University. All X-ray plates were examined there and no dog could be used for breeding unless it reached the required standard. Facha had passed; the problem was to find a sire who could equal her quality. Eventually she was mated to Brutus v. Georgshof, a dog which had repeatedly qualified at work and whose hips met with the approval of the Dutch examiners. In 1974 we flew over to Amsterdam to see her litter. We chose two: a dog, Torro Triomfator, and a bitch, Tara Triomfator. Mated to Borgvaale Venus, Torro produced a dog we have already mentioned, Ch. Chesara Dark Roisterer, and to Lucky Thirtry of Upend, Mrs Barbara Butler's Ch. Upend Gallant Gairbert. Tara mated to Christals Rebel of Alastel gave us Chesara Dark Herod. Herod, as we have already said, sired Ch. Chesara Dark Charles, plus four other champions. No one could ever claim that Herod was a beautiful-looking dog. He did not, however, have any obvious faults and we had the feeling that he could be a powerful stud force.

If you care to re-read the preceding paragraphs you will realize that Charles is the result of line-breeding to very carefully selected stock. All those qualities which he has passed on to his descendants are concentrated in him. In 1983 Charles won the award for top stud dog all breeds. In other words he sired more Challenge Certificate winning dogs than any other stud dog in any other breed. In the preceding two years his father Herod had, on the same basis, been the top Rottweiler stud dog. In 1984 and 1985 Charles continued as the top Rottweiler stud dog. In 1986 his son, Mrs Vi Slade's Ch. Caprido Minstrel of Potterspride, was top Rottweiler stud dog. Over six years, three dogs, father, son, grandson.

The breeding of an outstanding dog cannot be purely a matter of external beauty. If such a dog is to be used to create future generations then he must be sound from a heredity point of view as well as in his actual appearance. Hip dysplasia has always been an important subject for Rottweiler breeders in Britain. Let us say straight away that we do not consider that H.D. is a major problem in the breed. Big breeds tend to suffer from this condition more

Rintelna the Bombardier C.D.Ex., U.D.Ex., sire of the first British
Champion

Rintelna the Bombardier tracking

Jan. The only known photograph of a Rottweiler in Britain during the years
1939–45

International and Dutch Champion Facha Triomfator – dam of the two
imports Toro and Tara Triomfator from Chesara

The first two British Rottweiler Champions (1966), handled by the authors
(C.M. Cooke)

Author with an early litter. One of these puppies was the first Rottweiler to
win a working puppy group

Ch. Chesara Dark Soliloquy. First Rottweiler to win a working group at a championship show

than the small ones, but the incidence of crippling H.D., as opposed to the existence of the condition in a dog who leads a perfectly normal life, is low. Furthermore, there are a number of cases of dogs who have been diagnosed as suffering from H.D. who have, for the whole of their lives, worked successfully in working trials. One such dog, X-rayed at eighteen months of age and again at six years old, showed no change in the condition of his hips over the whole of the period. In spite of the excellent quality of the dog and his very obvious intelligence, the dog was never bred from because of the diagnosis of H.D. at the first X-ray. This we consider to have been a mistake.

The first British H.D. scheme was an 'all or nothing' grading. Either a dog was clear or it failed. This was modified to allow a small degree of latitude by the introduction of the 'breeder's letter', roughly equivalent to what we now call a score of 5 to 12. Even when modified the scheme was very little help to breeders. Great claims were made for dogs with a breeder's letter, even greater claims for those with a BVA/K.C. H.D. certificate. There was no indication of how the dog stood in relation to others in the breed or to the overall level of H.D. in Rottweilers. Breeders owe a great debt to Dr Malcolm Willis, who argued for the introduction of the scoring scheme, and then allowed Rottweiler clubs to join the scheme which he had introduced for GSDs, for recording and analysing the resultant figures. Under this scheme it is possible to make comparisons of the hip conditions of different dogs and to compare a dog's score with the breed average. At the time of writing the Rottweiler breed average is a score of about fourteen. For a breeder to know that his dog is better or worse than the average for the breed is obviously of great value.

For many years we had used check X-rays without putting them through the scheme. Our main basis for selection was, did the dog move correctly, could it run, jump and stand up to rough and tumble games? Did it ever show signs of stiffness or lameness? We also paid attention to X-ray results. Herod's great-grandfather was Lars v.d. Hobertsburg, whom we have already mentioned for his soundness. Herod's grandfather was Ch. Jentris Gerontius who achieved a BVA/K.C. H.D. certificate. So did Herod's father, Christals Rebel of Alastel. When the scoring scheme came in we decided to score Herod who was then seven years old. He scored 0.0. Charles in his turn scored 0.0 and his son Ch. Caprido Minstrel of Potterspride also scored 0.0. We thus had five dogs in a straight descending line all scoring 0.0 or its earlier equivalent, achieved, in our opinion, by initially breeding from sound stock and confirmed by the scoring scheme.

Returning to the progress of the breed, 1975 saw the importation by the late Gordon McNeill of Ausscot Hasso von Marchenwald. As a serving soldier in Germany, Gordon fell in love with the Rottweiler and in particular with Hasso. Both man and dog enjoyed life to the full and adored each other. Any show where they were present was always a delight. Gordon made Hasso into a champion and Hasso left his mark as the sire of five champions, including the very lovely English and Canadian Champion Ausscot Cover Girl.

From the beginning of the seventies we started to see top winning Rottweilers who were several generations removed from their imported ancestors. Breeders continued to import but, at the time of writing, no later import has made any major impression on the breed. One or two have even had a detrimental effect. It is important to realize that a dog is not automatically good because he or she is imported. Importing is expensive and some breeders have attempted to recoup their costs by extravagant claims as to the quality of their imports.

In any study of the breed, mention must be made of Ch. Rudi Anton Bali. During the early eighties this dog won over thirty Challenge Certificates, four working groups, a best-in-show at a general championship show and a number of other awards. Expertly handled by Pat Bryant he established a breed record which will be hard to beat. However, at the time of writing, he has shown little ability to pass on his qualities to his offspring.

Parallel with the development of the Rottweiler in Britain was the growth of clubs catering for the breed. While there are those who believe that the best way to serve a breed is for one club to control everything, others believe that its interests are best served by a number of clubs. Competition between them invariably raises the standard of individual clubs. A number of clubs allows for a greater freedom of action for those who may not agree with the policy of existing clubs. Furthermore, the enormous growth in popularity meant that it was essential to have clubs serving different areas. Any one club soon has difficulty in catering for the interests of its members if they are scattered all over the country.

The second national club for the breed, The British Rottweiler Association, was formed in 1970. This was followed in 1977 by the Midland Rottweiler Club and subsequently by the Northern, the Scottish, the Northern Ireland, the Welsh and the Eastern Counties Rottweiler Clubs and the South Western Rottweiler Association. It is likely that still more will be formed in the near future.

As we have seen, in the early sixties there were probably around one hundred Rottweilers in Britain. During 1975 four hundred and one were registered at the Kennel Club. In 1986 the number registered during the year exceeded 8000, making it the third most popular dog in the working group. To those of us who started at the beginning it is gratifying that so many people have joined us in our love for the breed. It is also heartbreaking to see the results of the exploitation of the Rottweiler by those whose sole interest is in making money from the breed, and who have no scruples in harming the Rottweiler for their own gain.

4

Your Rottweiler Puppy

Whether you are buying your Rottweiler as a puppy or choosing one from a litter you have bred yourself, the same factors will govern your decision. If you are the breeder you will have the advantage of being able to spend several weeks studying the litter before making your choice. If you are buying your puppy you will only have a maximum of an hour or so to choose and, in fact, you may have no choice at all. Many breeders will have sorted out the litter beforehand and made their own decisions as to which puppy will fill each purchaser's requirements. You may be told that 'this is the puppy you may have' and the inference is that if you do not want him then you will not have one at all. Do not be annoyed by this attitude. Provided that you are dealing with reputable breeders they will have assessed each puppy's potential, both physically and in temperament, against their assessment of you as an owner and your requirements. In fact, the breeder who shows you a whole litter and announces that you may take any one you wish is probably very short of potential customers, and has no more knowledge than you of the quality of each individual puppy. The term 'pick of litter' is sometimes used. To dog people this means the best puppy in the whole litter. It does not mean, as has been interpreted by some beginner breeders, that the whole litter can be sold as 'pick of litter' on the grounds that each purchaser in turn has the choice of whatever puppies are still unsold.

Advertisements of puppies for sale are often couched in glowing terms. Like all advertisements they should be read with considerable scepticism. It is highly unlikely that an entire litter is of show quality. Even the best breeders consider themselves lucky if they get two or three out of a large litter with show potential. Furthermore, if breeders are sensible and honest, they will only claim that a seven- or eight-week-old puppy has show potential at that time. Many a promising puppy changes as he matures and there is also the very real problem of inexperienced or inefficient rearing. The top breeders probably do not advertise at all. Their reputation is such that they can sell all they produce without the need to do so.

Assuming that you do not have a litter of puppies sitting in your whelping-box to choose from, where do you start? The dog papers carry advertisements of stock for sale, and the Kennel Club issues a list of breeders under the title of Kennel Index. A word of warning about the Kennel Index. Although it is used by the Kennel Club in response to enquiries for stock, it does not in any way carry a Kennel Club recommendation as to quality. Any person owning an affix can, by paying the requisite fee, have their name included in the Kennel Index. The same care should be applied to affixes. Although there have been what are, in our opinion, very desirable attempts to make the affix into an indication of quality, the fact is that a Kennel Club affix is available to any person willing to pay the fee. No other qualifications are required. Some Rottweiler breed clubs include a list of breeders in their newsletters and yearbooks. Again, they are only a form of paid advertising and do not carry any recommendation from the breed clubs concerned.

You will, of course, use all these sources as aids in your search for a puppy. They will give you names, addresses, telephone numbers and help you to locate breeders. You will notice that we have only mentioned breeders as a source of a puppy. You may be tempted to buy from a pet shop or a dealer. There are a number of people making a living out of dealing in puppies. We can think of no reason why you should buy your puppy from such a source and many reasons why you should not. Puppies offered by dealers will probably have been transported a considerable distance under miserable conditions at a time when they are susceptible to trauma and disease. They may have been kept, while awaiting sale, in insanitary kennels and at the risk of infection. The dealer will not offer any after sale service and will almost certainly have little specialist knowledge of Rottweilers and, therefore, be unable to advise you. You will be unable

to see the parents of your puppy, there is a possibility that
the pedigree will be inaccurate and you may have difficulty
in obtaining Kennel Club registration. There is always a risk
that you will buy the dear little cuddly bundle in order to
remove him from the conditions under which he is being
kept. We can only remind you that if you do he will
immediately be replaced by another one.

If you have decided that a Rottweiler is what you want you
will probably have seen one owned by a friend or neighbour.
If you have fallen for the breed as a result, then you should
ask where they got him, and even more important who his
parents are and who bred him. You may very well find that
you have a reputable breeder in your area and your search
may stop there. However, whether you want a puppy for
show or as a pet the best place to see the breed in quantity is
at a dog show. Pet owners may not realize that there is
almost certainly a dog show, within a reasonable distance
from their home, nearly every weekend. A copy of the *Kennel
Gazette* will give you details of all shows to be held for the
next six months.

Dog shows provide you with the opportunity to see both
dogs and breeders in the flesh and a little time spent watching and listening will soon give you a picture of those
breeders who are successful and, more importantly, have a
reputation for fair play. A copy of the show catalogue will
give their names and addresses and also the breeder and
breeding of any dog which catches your eye.

Whilst shows are a good place to make your first contact
and ask questions, they are usually busy times for the
exhibitors and they cannot always answer all the questions
you will wish to ask, simply because they are rushing into the
ring with another young hopeful. Do not be upset if
exhibitors are a little short-tempered and edgy if you
approach them just as they enter the ring. Showing dogs is
an emotive business and many exhibitors, however experienced, go through all the stress of an actor about to go on
stage when they take their dog into its class.

Having decided which breeder produces the sort of
Rottweiler you are looking for, the next stage is to discuss
your requirements with them. Do telephone for an appointment. Kennels are not shops which are open all hours. You

will wish to spend some time discussing your needs and it is only fair to pick a time convenient for the breeder.

If you are a married couple we suggest that both of you make this visit. If you have children then take them along to see if they are suitably well behaved with dogs. It is not unusual for the husband to be enthusiastic at the thought of a large male Rott while his wife retreats into the car, shuts all the doors and says, 'don't you bring that great brute near me'. In all probability she will be the one who has to be with the puppy for most of the day, cleaning up behind him, feeding him, and saving his life when he decides to chew through the vacuum cleaner cord. When he is fully grown she will have to protect the postman and take the dog for exercise. Breeders will not be at all keen to sell a puppy to a household where it is likely to cause domestic strife. They know from experience that eventually it will be a case of 'either the dog goes or I do' and almost invariably it is the Rott that has to go back to mother. So be sure that both of you are aware and happy about what you are taking on. Do not dress up as if you were going to a cocktail party. You are going to see dogs. Most breeders can tell stories of rejecting prospective owners because they spent their time complaining of laddered stockings or muddy paw marks on their suits. Incidentally, if the breeder does not reject you for these reasons he is probably not a conscientious breeder worried about the welfare of his puppies. Do not be surprised or annoyed if you are given a very thorough interrogation as to your previous experience with other dogs, circumstances, strength of character, size of house and garden and even whether your marriage is likely to break up. Once again the breeder wishes to ensure that his carefully reared puppy is going into the right sort of home where he will stay for the rest of his life. In return the breeder should be prepared to give you what is called 'supportive after sales service', which means that he is available to offer advice, assess the puppy's progress when you take him back to see him, and listen with pleasure and interest when you spend half an hour on the telephone in the middle of a busy day telling him all the wonderful, or awful, things your puppy has done.

On this, your first visit, you should try and get the answers to all your questions. The breeder will go to endless trouble to help someone who really wants to acquire knowledge. You should be able to see adult stock and the conditions under which the dogs are kept. If, on this visit, you are actually looking at young puppies you should be able to see their dam. Treat with a certain amount of suspicion the litter whose dam is not available. It probably means that the seller has bought in a litter for resale or indulges in the questionable practice of farming out bitches for breeding. To be fair there may be a legitimate reason for the absence of the bitch but find out for your own protection what it is.

It is not unusual if the sire of the litter is not available. He may be if the breeder has used one of his own stud dogs. If so, ask to see him. However, it is quite probable that the breeder has used someone else's stud dog. Ask who he is; he may be a dog that you have already seen or heard of. Remember that he represents one half of your prospective puppy's parentage.

Do not pretend to know more than you do. Just because a friend of your wife's first cousin once won first prize at the dog show held with the local fête, you are not necessarily a dog expert. Neither will you be popular if, when talking to a famous breeder, you ask whether their dogs are bred from so and so, naming a minor breeder who bought his first Rottweiler three years ago.

If, after these preliminaries, both you and the breeder are happy with each other, then it is time to talk about booking a puppy. You may have to go on a waiting list, especially if you require a show quality puppy. Be patient; it should be well worth waiting for.

You will probably not be allowed to see the puppies until they are about four weeks old. Frankly, before this, there is not a lot to see. A collection of black blobs tucked in close to their mother who would probably object to your presence. By four weeks the puppies are becoming individuals and it is possible to start making a preliminary choice. If it is your own home-bred litter you will, of course, have been handling and evaluating them from the day they were born. At four weeks, in a good litter, the puppies should be short-backed, square, sturdy, 'bear-like' little creatures. Their coats will be rather woolly. They do not become smooth and shiny until about ten weeks. They should be clean and free from any offensive smell. Most dog people love the smell of a healthy baby puppy.

It is really a waste of time trying to make a final decision at this age. We have already explained why you may get little or no choice and we would be very surprised if at eight weeks you were able to identify out of eight or ten puppies the one you chose at four weeks.

If, on your visit, you decide to take the children with you, and there is no reason why not, please do not expect that they will be allowed to handle or play with the puppies. Infection is always a risk with a young litter. Do not arrive at the kennels announcing that you have just been looking at another litter, visiting the stray dogs' home or that the next door neighbour's dog died of parvovirus last night. Help the breeders by not running any risk of taking in someone else's germs.

When the day arrives for you to collect your puppy we suggest that you take a passenger with you. The best place for a puppy to travel is on the lap of a passenger equipped with several clean newspapers and a towel or blanket. Travelling on a person's lap helps to reassure the puppy and decreases the chance of his being car-sick. If you have to make a solo journey then take a proper cage or travelling box. New owners often arrive with a shallow cardboard box complete with blanket and are surprised to find that the puppy is out of the box and under their feet before they have driven out of the kennel gate. Neither should a baby puppy be left to rattle around in the back of an estate car, and he certainly should not be shut in the boot, as an unsuccessful prospective purchaser once wanted to do with one of ours.

Before you leave to collect your new baby you will have made preparations for his homecoming. Decide where he is going to sleep and have some sort of bed ready. Remember that he will be used to the comfort and warmth of his litter mates. Whether your puppy is going to be a family companion or the start of your Rottweiler kennel, we like our puppies to be brought up in the house. Having the puppy indoors you can watch his development and socialize him, getting him used to domestic noises and visitors. For a number of years we have used the cage system for puppies living indoors. We have a number of these of different sizes but we suggest that you use one that is big enough for an adult. It must be a weld mesh cage that allows its occupant to see and hear what is going on around him. A box or tea chest fitted with a door will not do. The cage allows you to shut the puppy away when you are doing housework or entertaining non-doggy visitors. It also ensures that he will sleep safely at night without chewing the furniture. We find that young adults will continue to use the cage as their bed even with the door open. Newspaper on the floor will mean that cleaning up is made easy rather than involving searching behind the furniture to discover where he has decided to deposit his little heaps. Obviously time in the cage is kept to the minimum. Ours are let out at every possible opportunity and any visitor to our home is used as an opportunity to socialize our latest.

At long last you have made the final decision. This is the puppy which is either going to be your companion for the rest of his life or the one which will achieve for you your life long ambition to own a champion. What should he look like?

At eight weeks your puppy will weigh approximately 14 to 15 lbs, depending on sex, with a rounded chunky body and very thick strong legs. Avoid any thin, weak-boned puppy as these rarely grow into substantial adult Rottweilers. Do not, however, miss the finer-boned, more dainty one, who may be a little smaller but full of spirit and with a jaunty movement and clean-cut outline. Especially if you are looking for a bitch this one may grow up to be the best of the lot.

A litter bred from show-winning parents will probably not show as great a divergence between the show specimen and the pet, but there are certain points to look for if a show puppy is required, and here the experienced breeder can be of the greatest help. Look for good-boned, straight front legs with strong arched toes. The brisket should be quite well developed. The top line or back should be short and level. If he looks long in the loin at this age, he will be long in the back as an adult. This applies to the croup which, if it appears to slope at this age, will rarely improve. Look for a reasonable bend of stifle and hocks that are not too long. If the puppy looks slightly 'cow-hocked', this can improve as he grows, but if these turned-out feet are pronounced, there will not be sufficient drive, and the resulting weak movement will be penalized in the show ring. Clear rich tan markings are desirable and a good dense coat. The head is the most difficult part to judge at this age, since maturity brings very great changes, not always for the better, but certain characteristics may be assessed. Basically, the head is shaped like a blunt-ended triangle viewed from above; the ears form a continuation and give width to the top line of the skull and should not be too large. Avoid a puppy with too much loose skin and wrinkle on the head, particularly around the eyes, as the eye should be tight-set, of a good dark colour and not too full. The muzzle on a puppy should not look narrow and pointed, nor be so square as to resemble a Bull Mastiff. The front teeth must close over the lower teeth. This is known as a scissor bite, but if there is a slight gap between the teeth in this position, and the important word is 'slight', this will close when the adult teeth arrive. If, however, the teeth are almost edge to edge, there is a very strong likelihood of this puppy becoming undershot when mature. In our experience, an undershot mouth rarely improves, and such a puppy should not be sold as a future show or breeding prospect.

If you are buying a show puppy the above description is what you are looking for. In a companion puppy you may have to accept that not everything is perfect. A tiny spot of white on the chest is quite common and is purely a cosmetic fault. In most cases it will eventually fade into the tan but will persist if it is solid colour right through to the skin. Tan markings may be paler than the ideal. Again, it makes no difference to the future of the dog as a companion. You must also remember that you should be paying less for one that has not reached potential show quality. If you must have the perfect one as a pet then you must pay for him. If the breeder will sell him.

Although we have discussed the minor physical differences between pets and show pups, there is one aspect which has not yet been mentioned which is by far the most important, and that is the temperament of the puppy. This is of the same importance no matter what kind of pup you want. If the puppy has been handled and talked to since his earliest days, he will be pleased to see visitors, and there is no more delightful sight to see than a litter of puppies waking from sleep and joyfully tumbling out of their box and rushing to greet you. Most Rottweiler pups are lively, inquisitive little extroverts and this naughty type of character is easier to cope with ultimately. The shy, aloof puppy is usually over-sensitive, and a quiet, sheltered life is more suited to his nature than being a family or show dog. So choosing your puppy means looking, listening and learning and, finally, loving the one you take home.

With your puppy the breeder should give you a diet-sheet suggesting how your puppy should be fed for the next few weeks. We also like to give a sufficient amount of the food he has been having to last at least 48 hours. This gives time for the new owners to obtain their own supply. Whatever ideas you may have about puppy rearing we suggest that you follow the breeder's advice at first. The puppy has enough to cope with, new people, new house, new noises, without upsetting his tummy with a new diet.

You should also receive from the breeder a copy of your puppy's pedigree and Kennel Club registration certificate, but as this takes some time to come through you may have to wait until it is posted to you. The breeder should give you details of when the puppy was wormed, and if he has been inoculated a certificate giving details and the date. They will also, we hope, give you a final briefing on your particular puppy and an invitation to contact them if you have any problems.

The puppy should have been getting four meals a day, probably two based on meat and biscuit and two based on milk and cereal. Supplements, as we have already said, should be used sparingly. Too much can do a lot of harm. At about four months you can reduce the number of meals to three and at six months to two.

Food quantities are important. As with weaning, food should be put down, eaten, and the surplus, if any, taken away. It should not be left with the puppy to become stale, fly-blown and uninteresting. Constant access to food is a method for battery hens, not Rottweilers. While we urge you to stick to a laid-down diet, this does not mean that you should not feed the occasional titbit. Chocolate drops, bits of cheese, liver or small dog biscuits shoud be used as a reward for good behaviour and as a pleasure shared between you. Povided that your puppy is growing well and is neither too fat nor too thin then you are getting it right. We are often asked whether a puppy is too fat or too thin. The simplest test is that you should be able to feel the ribs but not see them.

Serious training should start at about six months of age and we cover this in Chapter 5, 'Living with a Rottweiler'. However, although you do not tell your puppy this, his training starts from the moment he arrives at your home. Start by letting him find out for himself what a marvellous home he has come to. Let him explore in his own time both your house and the people in it. Incidentally, his arrival is a time when everybody in the family wants to make a fuss of him. He may immediately respond and love all the attention. On the other hand he has had a long tiring journey, everything is strange and he needs time to adjust. So do not overpower him on his first arrival and, much as the children will want to get to know him, please restrain them for a little while.

We have one basic rule in training a puppy. It is quite simple. Never let the puppy do anything that you would not want him to do as an adult. It is unfair to expect him to understand that something he was allowed to do when he weighed 20 lbs is forbidden when he weighs 120 lbs. That said, because we allow our adults to jump up at us and give us loves we do not stop it in our puppies. We enjoy their display of affection. If you do not, then do not allow it when he is a puppy. The first command our puppies learn is 'no', which means 'whatever you are doing stop it'. 'No' is a nice short word that you can spit out in a cross voice or murmur in a calm admonition. Our second command is 'wait'. This means that I am going through this door and you are staying on the other side of it and not pushing your way through. You will find that these two commands, and they can be learnt very quickly at an early age, make life a lot easier. The third lesson is for him to learn his name. We should explain that your Rottweiler will have a Kennel Club registered name which will be chosen by the breeder. You will probably have thought of a name after much family discussion, and the choice is obviously yours. You will wish to choose what most people call a 'kennel name': the name you use when speaking to the puppy. The kennel name may be part of its registered name but as this is likely to be something like 'Bootlesboots Thunderblitz' you will probably prefer something handier. When you choose a kennel name there are a few points to remember. It should be short, sharp, not likely to be confused with the names of other dogs that you own, and something that you are not embarrassed to shout out at the top of your voice. A friend of ours once named a pair of bulldogs with two rather vulgar obscenities. Everyone thought it was funny until they ran away from her in the middle of a crowded High Street. Everyone, except her, still thought it was funny.

Use your puppy's name whenever you can. Associate it with food, special titbits and signs of affection. He will rapidly identify with it.

If you are planning a show career for your Rott do not allow anyone to teach him to sit. In-laws, children and visitors with memories of the family pet will invariably spend hours teaching your hopeful to sit for a biscuit. He will learn all right and show you how well he has learnt by insisting on sitting down, to please you, in the middle of the show ring. The obedience trainers will tell you that it is just a question of teaching the dog to stand on command. Quite true, but an obedience stand is inclined to be a slight crouch, head turned awaiting the next command. In the show ring you want an alert dog staring across the ring, head up and body tensed. If you intend to do both beauty and obedience then you will just have to put up with it; many people do, quite successfully, but it makes life difficult. If you set out to do both, teach a show stand first.

House-training, or teaching your puppy to be clean, is a subject which will have a high priority for obvious reasons. Rottweilers, unlike some of the toy breeds, learn cleanliness very quickly. The floor of the whelping room was probably covered in newspaper, and from the time he was able to walk he would have had the natural instinct to leave the actual bed and go on to the newspaper. Using newspaper soon becomes a habit and a piece placed on the kitchen floor will soon be used when required. The use of newspaper has the disadvantage that it is unwise to put the Sunday paper on the floor alongside your chair until you are quite sure that you have finished reading it. Leaving this aside, your puppy should be given every encouragement to be clean by being put outside first thing in the morning, last thing at night, after every meal and on every occasion in between when he shows signs of wanting to go to the door. Effusive praise should be given for every successful visit to the garden and utter disgust expressed for every failure while indoors. Do not indulge in smacking or rubbing his nose in it. He has not the slightest idea of what he has done wrong.

You must learn to make your commands to your puppy in a tone which expresses your meaning. Clever as they are, Rottweilers do not speak English or any other language at eight weeks of age, although they will eventually learn quite a few words. 'No', given in a friendly tone of voice, may mean 'no' to you, but it will not necessarily be understood by the puppy purely because of its spelling and pronunciation. The first 'no' when he misbehaves should be firm and clear; the second, if he persists in his misdemeanour, should be an explosion of rage. Listen to a Rottweiler bitch telling off her litter with ferocious snarls. She will not harm them but she makes it very clear that she does not approve of what they are doing. Learn to do the same. You should never actually lose your temper with a dog but you must be able to give a very good impression that you have done so. A puppy has no hands to grip with. He uses his mouth for those actions which you will use your hands for. In the same way that a human baby starts to grip and thus discover the use and limitations of his hands, a puppy will use his mouth and teeth to find out and test his ability. It is not unusual for first time owners to complain that their eight-week-old Rottweiler has bitten them in the ankle and drawn blood. It must, therefore, be vicious and will the breeder take it back immediately. All our eight-week-old puppies bite us on the ankle. None of them have grown up into vicious adults. The puppy is merely learning what he can do with his mouth and your ankle happens to be handy. The answer is to teach him that your reaction to this is to be cross. He will have no desire to make you cross and will soon learn not to do it again.

We have already said that physical violence to an adult

Rottweiler is self-defeating and should play no part in his training or control. The same does not apply to a puppy. No dog, whatever his age, should be beaten, but a quick smack, probably with only two fingers, on the part of the puppy which has given offence will be both remembered and effective. If he bites your ankle then tap him smartly on the nose at the same time as you let out your anguished yell of 'NO!' Some people will tell you that smacking a dog on the head will make it 'hand-shy'. We have never found this to be true but it probably only happens two or three times in his life. Such retribution must be immediate. An admonition given half-an-hour after the offence will not be related to its cause, and will leave the puppy wondering why you have apparently suddenly taken leave of your senses.

Do not nag at your puppy. Offence, retribution and all over and back to normal is the rule. Smacking should rarely be necessary: most of your training should come from commands and the tone in which they are given.

One final point on this subject. Praise for successfully carrying out your wishes is even more important than punishment for failing to do so. Praise and encouragement should be used all the time, and do not be embarrassed if you find yourself giving out words of encouraging baby talk in public. Your Rottweiler will appreciate them and understand, even if others do not.

Lead training can start at about ten weeks. Use a very small and cheap collar; he will grow out of it very fast and you will probably need two or three before he is big enough to wear the strong choke chain and lead that you bought for him. At first let him wear the collar, without the lead, adjusted so that you can get one finger inside it. Some puppies will immediately go into a decline, sitting in a corner unable to move because of the thing you have put around their neck. Most Rotts will have a couple of scratches and then ignore it. Either way, leave it on and let him get used to wearing it. The next stage is to attach a very light lead and let it trail for a few minutes. Stay around, otherwise he will promptly chew your new lead into three-inch pieces. Pick up the lead and let him lead you. Do not immediately apply pressure or allow the lead to tighten. Just follow him around. At this stage he is taking you for a walk. Gradually the fact that he is attached to you by this length of leather will sink in. Very slowly start to persuade him to follow you. Use titbits to encourage him. If he panics and pulls back, go with him. Panic followed by the sudden pull on his neck will only increase his fear. Keep at it until he trots happily with you. An older dog on a lead alongside you often encourages the puppy to follow but this is best done with two people, one with the older dog and one with the puppy. Attempts to control both dogs by one person can result in the puppy becoming frightened, and you being unable to move to calm him down.

If you plan to show your puppy then training to stand in the ring can commence at three to four months. Almost all exhibitors use food as 'bait'. The art of baiting with food is to give as little bait as possible but to stretch out the anticipation for as long as you can. Start by telling the puppy to stand while waving your tasty piece of liver under his nose. The moment he does any sort of a stand with all four legs on the ground give him the liver and lots of praise. Two or three minutes a day spent on this training is quite sufficient. Never give him the reward unless he is standing. Never reward, however appealing he may be, if he is sitting, standing on his hind legs or tearing the liver pocket out of your coat. Gradually stretch out the anticipation. Your hand should fumble, half slide out of the pocket and return until, just when the Rott is about to explode with frustration, he gets his reward. All right, so some say it is just greed on the part of the Rottweiler, but he certainly looks good to the judge as he stands there alert and taut with anticipation.

Up to the age of eight weeks, exercise for your puppy will have consisted of games with his litter mates, firstly in the whelping box and then in the attached run. From then on when the puppy is living on his own he should still be allowed to exercise at his own discretion up to at least three months. This does not preclude the occasional introduction to a collar and lead. The important point is that the puppy should not be dragged out for walks, probably on hard pavements and for a greater distance than is desirable. Even though it may not fit your routine, if the puppy is sleeping let him sleep. When he wakes up and wants to play, then take time to play with him. Resist the desire of members of the family to wake him up for games or a walk. The aim is sleep interspersed with short periods of games. Gradually, he will spend less time sleeping and more time playing. Even adult dogs will spend a large part of their time sleeping, if allowed to, and puppies require even more. At this stage you can start to take him for short walks, but remember: although he may be growing quite large he is still only a baby.

Toys are very necessary for a puppy. He has the need to chew on things, especially when teething. A single puppy lacks the litter mates to play and tussle with that he would have in the wild. He will enjoy throwing a toy around, catching it and destroying it. If you do not provide toys he will would have in the wild. He will enjoy throwing a toy around, catching it and destroying it. If you do not provide toys he will help himself, probably to your best slippers. Pet shops have lots of dog toys, many of which are designed to appeal to you rather than your dog. A thick marrow bone will keep a puppy amused for hours. Ours are given empty cardboard cartons, soft plastic empty bottles, which make a lovely noise when thrown around, or the odd old slipper or shoe. Do please check that whatever he has cannot be broken into sharp splinters or bite-sized dangerous pieces. Rubber balls can sometimes be chewed into small pieces and swallowed. Balls must be of a size that cannot be swallowed, or more likely, become stuck in the throat. Nylon stockings are lethal as they can be swallowed, not digested, and then block the intestine. Buttons are favourite objects for a puppy to swallow and can be fatal. The hide chews sold for dogs will keep them happy for hours but be careful; steady chewing by a Rottweiler will soften them until pieces can be swallowed, and if so, your puppy will have an upset tummy to say the least.

Car-sickness in dogs is similar to that in humans. Some are and some are not. It can become psychological so that the dog starts drooling and feeling sick even before the car has moved. From a very early age you should take your puppy out for short drives, preferably with the puppy in the lap of a passenger. Should the puppy look uncomfortable a quick word and a cuddle to take his mind off it will often avert sickness.

Diversion or distraction is always a useful aid in puppy training and for adults as well. A waved toy, a word of endearment or a titbit can take the dog's mind off something you do not want him to do, and channel it into another interest. On many occasions it is better than a reprimand, achieving your object without a confrontation.

Puppy days are happy days. Enjoy them. A puppy growing up will give you many hours of pleasure plus a few of exasperation, while at the same time you help him to evolve in the way you wish.

5

Living with a Rottweiler

Many people just wish to own a dog as a companion, as a much loved part of the family and in many cases as a guard as well. The Rottweiler fits superbly into this role and while the keen breeder/exhibitor may complain about a good dog wasted in a pet home, there is really no finer life for a Rott than this. It is almost invariably the pet Rottweiler who gives rise to all the stories of the extraordinary and loveable things that they do. There is no reason why the dog who goes into a family as a companion should not be a good specimen of the breed, both in temperament and physical appearance. In fact, for the good name of the breed, it is very desirable that he should be so. In the long run it is the image of the breed held by the general public which makes or mars its reputation.

The Rott is a very adaptable dog. He likes nothing better than joining in your activities. We know of a Rottweiler who flies with his owner in his own private plane. Air traffic controllers are slightly shattered to see a Rottweiler sitting in the co-pilot's seat. Others go sailing or swimming. Several farmers have them with them all day riding in the cab of the tractor. One farmer we know, who uses a three-wheeled motor-cycle as a runabout on the farm, has taught his Rott to ride on a small platform at the back, ready to dismount and herd sheep. There are Rotts who act as retrievers for rough shooting. If you like long walks a Rott is the ideal companion. He will even go fishing with you and perhaps catch a bigger one than you can!

He will fit into life in a town provided that you make the effort to see that he gets reasonable exercise. One we know was brought up as a puppy in a very luxurious London flat filled with valuable glass and china. His owner claimed that he had never broken or damaged a single item. More than she could claim for her housekeeper. Another is the regular companion and protector of a district nurse whose duties take her out at night.

The Rottweiler will enjoy combining companionship with work. One bitch worked for her whole life with a security officer for London Transport. Checking double-decker buses in the garage, she would rest her muzzle on the bottom step of the stairs, which was sufficient to tell her whether anyone was hiding on the top deck. All clear and she would move on to the next bus. If there was someone hiding on top she would run up the stairs and escort them down. Another led an ideal life with a gamekeeper, living with the family all day and at night on duty patrolling the woods with his master.

The first decision you have to make if you decide to share your life with a Rottweiler is whether it shall be dog or bitch. Some will solve the problem by deciding to have a pair. Our advice is to start with one, enjoy it, watch it develop, train it as you wish and then if you are quite sure, add your second one, which in our opinion should be of the opposite sex. Two young Rotts growing up in the house together can provide more problems than pleasure. We have already discussed the character of the Rottweiler. In making a decision between dog or bitch we would point out that bitches are just as intelligent, just as trainable, and just as faithful and efficient guards. They are, however, smaller than the males, not quite so convinced of their dominant place in the world and while they still believe in their superiority over all other dogs, are not quite so determined to prove it. If your own size, strength or age are relevant factors then a bitch may be the better choice for you. It may also be the better choice if this is your first experience of owning a large powerful breed.

Bitches, of course, come in season. While it is normally every six months, seasons can be more frequent. Seasons give you two problems. Firstly, if she lives indoors, she is going to leave bloody drops around the house for a period of some two to three weeks. She may also attract a number of 'gentlemen callers' who will sit on your front step with their tongues hanging out. The problem of drops of colour can be solved by keeping her for the duration of her season in a room with an easily cleaned floor, such as the kitchen or a utility room. She may not like it but she will just have to put up with it. The caller problem should be solved by owners keeping their dogs at home and not allowing them to roam the streets. Regrettably this does not always happen. So, you have to keep her safe and sound for something like six weeks out of the year. Should you find that you cannot manage to protect her during her seasons then you may consider spaying her. If you do decide to have her spayed, the usual veterinary advice is that it should not be done until after the first season. Some vets are now spaying much younger, at four to five months, and are of the opinion that this is satisfactory. Rescue kennels are using this method to prevent rehomed puppies being bred from. We have not had first-hand experience of this but would suggest that you leave it until after her first season. You should also insist that your vet advises you of any detrimental side effects as a result of spaying. One disadvantage is that some bitches become incontinent.

We have said that control of a Rottweiler, of either sex, is more mental than physical. Many women are perfectly capable of controlling a male by virtue of their own strength of character. Some of the closest relationships between Rottweilers and owners that we have known have been with women. Many of these Rotts have been males. They can be the most polished cavaliers with the ladies. Numbers of Rottweilers are the constant companions of women living alone who are probably better protected than can ever be achieved by the forces of law and order. Many a child plays happily and safely because part of the family is a Rott who considers the child his special care.

An acquaintance of ours has a Rottweiler bitch who is a great favourite. They have no children of their own and she has had very little contact with them. On this particular occasion the bitch was swimming in shallow water with a small boy alongside. Suddenly the child started screaming, while the bitch was barking and apparently attacking him. The owner dashed into the sea, brought out dog and child and scolded the bitch. The boy's mother, examining the child, discovered no dog bites but dozens of small red spots which were afterwards identified as stings from a large jellyfish, a 'Portuguese Man-of-War'. Far from attacking the child, the Rottweiler, although unused to children, was doing her best to defend him. Being a Rottweiler she accepted their apologies and forgave her owners for their lack of faith.

If you are content to have your Rottweiler purely as a companion, and nothing more, then we would never disagree. You may, however, wish to gain even more satisfaction from your companion by taking part in one or more of the many activities which have developed from man's association with the dog. Those who do take this further step will find that they gain great additional pleasure from their Rottweilers. These activities include dog shows, obedience competition, working trials and agility. There is also the very worthy cause known as P.A.T. dogs which exists to bring the happiness of a dog's companionship to people in hospitals, old people's homes and other places where the occasional visit of a well-behaved dog can brighten a long weary day.

All of these have the advantage that it is possible to start at a very low level in your own area and progress, if your enthusiasm takes hold, to major competitions, which include such events as Crufts, and agility, obedience and working trials up to championship level.

For those owners who from necessity or desire can only keep one, or at the most, two Rottweilers, we would strongly recommend that you consider agility, obedience or working trials rather than beauty showing. The show life of a dog in beauty is probably a maximum of about three years. It starts at six months in puppy classes and by the time the dog is three to four years old he has either won everything he can and is starting to be beaten by up-and-coming youngsters or, as is much more likely, you will have realized at about the age of eighteen months that your dog is not going to have a meteoric career as a show dog. When you reach this decision you then have the problem of what to do. You can of course stop showing and enjoy your Rott as the much loved companion he has always been. If, however, the show bug has bitten you, you are going to start looking for another one. If, as we have said, you can only keep one or two, what is going to happen to those who have failed to make the grade in the show ring and those who have done well for you but are now retired? The breeder/exhibitors with ample kennel space will, of course, consider putting the successful dogs at stud and breeding from the winning bitches. If they are sensible they will have found pet homes for those who do not make the grade at the earliest possible age. The ones who have served them well in the ring and for breeding will, we hope, be kept for the rest of their lives as kennel pensioners. Inevitably, if you go in for beauty showing you will have to be able to keep quite a number of dogs.

If your choice is work, your one dog can have a long life of competition at whatever level you are able to achieve. To a certain extent, whereas the show dog reaches it speak at about two and a half years of age, the working dog can continue to improve until old age makes his joints too stiff to continue.

There is no doubt in our minds that there is a great deal of satisfaction in having a Rottweiler as your constant companion whose ability at work is steadily developed by you. One has a great sense of pride and achievement in his or her ability, and the knowledge that working together has made your joint success possible. We can recall one such owner who collected his dog after boarding him whilst on holiday. He collected him at about 8 p.m. on a dark and wintry night with some 60 miles to go before he reached home. Talking to us a few days later he said that he decided to see whether his dog remembered his training. Stopping on a patch of empty heath he threw his car keys off into the long grass and told his dog to find them. The Rott immediately did so. This is what we really call mutual trust and confidence.

There are nearly 500 Kennel Club registered dog training societies and probably as many more unregistered ones. Although they vary in quality you should be able to find one within a few miles of your home. In addition most of the Rottweiler breed clubs run training classes. Although it may be easier to use a local all-breeds training club, some of the instructors are not as well informed on the Rottweiler as we would wish. However, most of them are knowledgeable on dog training in general and you will be given the basic instruction you require. One word of advice: do not let the instructor take the dog away from you in a demonstration of how to do it. Some instructors will use methods which will either destroy your dog's confidence or, in the case of many Rotts, the dog will resent the treatment. Ask the instructor to tell you what to do and then you do it with your dog.

You may decide for several reasons to send your Rott away for training. There are a number of excellent trainers who will do this for you. There are also some very bad ones who will charge you a lot of money for very little. Sending the dog away for training can occasionally be successful. Frequently, however, it results in a dog which obeys the trainer's commands perfectly but fails to respond to you when you get him home.

There is no doubt that the best approach is for you and your Rott to learn side by side. In any case you are going to have to do regular, preferably daily, training between your weekly classes. Five to ten minutes is adequate.

Even if you do not aspire to competition work, a reasonable level of basic obedience training is essential and well worthwhile. It will make your enjoyment of your dog all the greater.

Your first need for training is a suitable lead and choke chain. First the choke chain. Some owners do not like choke chains. The name itself sounds unpleasant and some variations that have been produced are decidedly cruel. However, the fact remains that there can come a time when you need the control a choke chain can give and when you need it you need it badly. The obvious occasion is when your perfectly behaved Rott is attacked by another dog. Being a Rott he will both defend himself and punish the attacker. So, he has won the fight, but do you really want him to kill the other dog? Although the Rott's blood is up, he is perfectly trained and should 'leave' on command. Maybe he will, but there is a limit to the provocation a Rottweiler will take. A choke chain gives you that last chance to exercise control. Properly used, as many trainers describe it, as a check chain rather than a choke, it need cause no discomfort to the dog. Do not leave the choke chain on your Rottweiler while he is in kennels or running loose unsupervised. The dog could easily jump, catch the chain on something and hang himself.

Although the fine-linked chains look very smart, you may find that the action of the links acts as a form of clipper and wears the hair away around the neck. For this reason we prefer the long-linked chains with links a little over one inch in length. Whatever type you use make sure that it is well made and strong with all joints welded.

The same applies to the lead. The clip should be strong and made of wrought metal. The clips made of bent tin are useless. The lead should be of good quality leather with adequate stitching. We prefer a lead of about 3 ft 6 in. to 4 ft in length. Nylon leads are strong but tend to cut into the hand. Some webbing leads are good and comfortable to handle. Whale hide, which had a vogue at one time, stretches and you find your dog getting farther and farther away until the lead breaks. Working enthusiasts tend to use leads which are an elaborate combination of extra clips, 'D' rings and yards of leather. We are sure they find them useful but it always appears to us that the prime function of such a lead is to hang it around your neck to show onlookers that yours is a working dog.

Two items of equipment which are of fairly recent introduction are, firstly, the long nylon cord lead contained in a plastic handle. The handle contains a button operated brake so that the length of lead can be controlled and the cord is wound around a spring-loaded drum in the handle so that it automatically shortens when the tension is taken off. While these leads are useful for teaching exercises such as the recall, we find the handles clumsy and uncomfortable. The second recent introduction is the Halti, an arrangement of light nylon straps in the form of a loose fitting muzzle with the lead attachment pointing towards the end of the dog's nose. When you pull the lead the dog's head is turned in the direction of the pull; the dog literally has to follow his nose. This certainly gives you control of a difficult dog but in our opinion does not aid in training. The device appears to be rather flimsy and a dog can use his paw to remove it. When we have used it we have continued to use a check chain attached to the lead as a reserve.

Whatever future you plan for your Rottweiler he will need to learn a few basic commands. These are, to walk at your side on a lead without pulling, to come when you call him, either to sit, stand or lie down on one spot and the 'whatever you are doing, stop it' which we have already suggested is the response to the word 'no'. A further desirable command is either 'leave' or 'give', used when you wish to take something away from the dog. The sight of your Rottweiler about to swallow a roll of banknotes or a dead rat will probably cause you to make an impulsive snatch to retrieve it. Don't. The dog has found this treasure and at that moment it is his and he may resent you taking it away. Ask him nicely. The command 'give', possibly combined with the offer of an alternative attraction, will allow you to remove the object without argument. Some owners extend this to the removal of food at the moment that the dish is put down, believing that such control is desirable. We do not agree. While we expect to be able to take food away from our Rotts if it becomes necessary, we do not like the idea of regular training involving the dog sitting patiently looking longingly at his dish until he is given permission to eat. We believe that such training can produce finicky feeders and prefer our dogs to look forward to their meals rather than suffer another training session. Certainly it would make us very bad-tempered if at the moment we were about to cut our steak someone took it away and made us sit patiently until they condescended to return it.

Decide in advance what words of command you are going to use and stick to them. You will confuse yourself and the dog if you use a number of different words for the same action. We once had an exception to this rule: a Rott bitch who would obey commands in either English or German, having been trained by a Swiss girl living in England. She was a very clever bitch and her trainer was an expert.

We will start off with walking to heel on the lead. It is usual for the dog to walk on your left side. So that you do not arrive at your first training class to be told that you have your choke chain upside down, a favourite comment by instructors to new arrivals, you should place it over the dog's head, assuming that the dog is on your left, so that as a continuation of the lead it goes over the top of the dog's neck, under the throat and back to the lead. Try it first on your wrist and you will soon work it out. If you put it on the other way round so that the continuation of the lead goes under the throat first, then it will not slacken off when you cease to pull on it. Most of us hold the end of the lead in the right hand allowing it to run through the left hand.

Position the dog on your left side, say his name to attract

his attention, give the command 'heel' and step off smartly, at the same time giving a gentle jerk to the lead. The first time you do this the dog will either pull forward and ahead of you, jump to one side or sit down and refuse to move. Try again, giving the command and following it up with encouraging noises and patting your left leg. As we said about lead training for your puppy, do not allow him to panic, gasping for breath and struggling against the chain.

The purpose of a choke chain is not, as sometimes appears to be the case, to choke the dog into submission. The intention is that the dog should learn that the slightest tightening of the chain is the forewarning of greater pressure. The aim to achieve is the dog walking alongside you with the lead slack. Only if he pulls ahead, to one side, or lags behind, do you give a quick jerk to remind him and then immediately slacken the lead again. Each time you jerk the lead repeat the command 'heel', and all the time he is walking correctly on a loose lead lavish all the praise and endearments on him that you can.

Keeping the lead taut, which is probably instinctive to you until you gain confidence, will only result in a competition to see which will fail first, your arm or the dog's determination, and knowing the Rott it will be your arm. Far too often one sees a red-faced owner hanging for dear life on the end of a tight lead, on the other end of which is a large Rott, eyes bulging and tongue hanging out. Before someone else says it we will admit it can happen to all of us at times.

Having got your dog moving at your side it is obviously desirable that you know how to stop. Otherwise you may finish up like Felix, the cat who kept on walking. If you have succeeded in getting your Rott to match his pace to yours so that he remains at your side without checking by the lead, he will stop when you do. Then say the dog's name and the command 'sit', but not if you are aiming for the show ring. Say 'stand' instead.

For your dog to stay in one place without you necessarily remaining with him, the most comfortable position is for him to lie down. The usual command is 'down'. Start the training before he gets too big. Holding the lead in one hand, put your hands on the dog's withers and rump and push him firmly down and towards his rear so that he goes into the sitting position and continues on into the down, using the command 'down' as you do so. When he tries to rise press down again and repeat the command. The moment he relaxes in the down position use lots of praise. Once he will go down and stay there on command you can walk to the end of the lead repeating the command every time he shows signs of moving. The next step is to lay the lead on the ground and slowly move a yard or so away, repeating the command every time he shows signs of moving. Do not praise while he is lying quietly in the down. His instinct will be to get up and come to you. Eventually you will be able to remove the lead, put him at the down and walk out of sight, although it will pay you to peer through the crack in the door until you are quite certain he is going to stay there.

Coming when you call is a question of making the dog understand that coming to you is a happy moment when you are glad to see him, show him lots of affection and probably give him a titbit. However exasperating he has been beforehand, the time when he comes to you is not the time for a reprimand. Unlike humans, who are stupid enough to come when called and then stand there while being admonished, the Rott has more sense. His attitude is going to be: 'If that's the way you're going to carry on, I'll stay away next time.' Some Rottweilers adopt the attitude that, although they are aware that you will be glad to see them, they are rather busy at the moment and will come when it suits them. You can sometimes solve this problem by turning your back on him and moving quickly away, and calling him in an excited tone, a move which may bring him running after you in case he loses you. If this fails then use a very long light line so that the dog can get quite a distance away. Call him with all the usual encouragements and if this does not work slowly reel him in, still calling and encouraging. Repeated enough times this should solve the difficulty. The long line can also be used to cure the dog who takes off at a gallop for the nearest horizon when released from the lead, deaf to all your calls. Wait until he is almost at the end of the line and then jerk. The sudden surprise of being halted in mid-flight is usually very effective. As this method can bring the dog down quite heavily it should only be used as a last resort and even then with great care.

We have only attempted to give you the basic needs as far

as training is concerned. There are many excellent books on training available, including some on advanced obedience and working trials. Use your breed club and local dog training club for practice and advice.

Do not be daunted by the task of training your Rott; as we have said, he is very biddable and anxious to please you. All you have to do is tell him in a way he will understand what it is that you require.

The Rottweiler has a great sense of fun, but equally is conscious of his own dignity. He will join you in games, albeit rough ones, tease you if the mood takes him, and can, at times, pretend to suffer from complete deafness. On the other hand, he has a very highly developed sense of dignity and takes the greatest exception to being laughed at or treated without the respect he deserves.

His intelligence and courage have made him attractive to police forces and other organizations requiring a highly trained guard dog. These characteristics are inherent in the breed and for a dog required to fit into the everyday life of a home, need no further development. You will find that your Rottweiler will show quite adequate guarding instincts that merely need to be controlled by simple obedience training, and unless you both need and are able to control a tough guard dog, you should resist any suggestion of encouraging aggression in your dog.

Wherever you live, please do not allow your Rottweiler uncontrolled access to roads and public areas. Even though he will not go far from home, if he decides to include the road in front of your house in his 'territory', you are not going to be popular with the neighbours. Not everybody loves dogs and some people are very frightened of them. Even if you do not like your neighbours, it will be the dog that suffers in the end. Owning a dog of this size, power and character carries considerable responsibility. It is a rare Rottweiler indeed who will turn into a 'rogue' dog. However, dog owners do have responsibilities, both to the community and to their dog. It is your responsibility to protect your dog from situations where his natural instincts will run contrary to the attitudes and needs of the human world around him. For example, if you live in a farming area, your dog may show his inherent instinct as a herding breed by trying to herd farm animals. To your dog, and perhaps to you, this instinct was born in him; to a farmer it could be sheep worrying, with all the penalties which the offence carries. At the same time many farmers have trained and channelled this instinct so that their Rottweiler is a useful member of the farm work force.

Two idiosyncrasies capable of being misinterpreted are the Rottweiler's habits of 'grinning' and 'talking'. Many Rottweilers will greet a friend with a display of teeth, which to the uninitiated could be slightly disconcerting, but which is merely intended by the dog to be a smile of recognition. Equally, numbers of Rottweilers will respond to a scratch behind the ear or a rub of the tummy with a rumbling growl or occasional half-bark which sounds fearsome but is really only an expression of pleasure. You may feel that it is difficult for the newcomer to Rottweilers to know the difference between a display of teeth and a roar of annoyance, and a grin and a grumble of pleasure but we think you will quickly learn to recognize the difference when you live with a Rottweiler.

6

The General Care of your Rottweiler

Be grateful that the Rottweiler is a very basic dog, close in many ways to his wild forefathers. The breed does not suffer from exaggerated breed points which in some breeds give health problems which are entirely man-made. There are however certain aspects of his physical characteristics which can give problems if not properly understood. A Rottweiler puppy is born very small relative to the final adult weight. Many breeds which are smaller than the Rottweiler when fully grown give birth to puppies as large as or even larger than Rottweilers. This means that the Rottweiler has a very rapid growth rate. He will double his birth weight each week for the first three weeks and continue to increase in size at the rate of half his weight per week for several weeks after that. By eight weeks he will probably weigh in the region of 14 to 15 lbs. This increase in weight on a body whose bone and muscle are not fully developed can cause orthopaedic problems which are not apparent until later in life. The fat, butter-ball puppy at 8 or 9 weeks, attractive as he may seem, is not always the one who will grow into a fit adult without lameness or similar problems. Neither, of course, is the skinny undernourished runt. The ideal is somewhere between the two.

Because of this problem of weight-gain before the bone and muscle frame is ready to support it, you should avoid allowing your puppy to skid on highly polished or wet floors or to jump from heights. It may be amusing to see your determined youngster clambering up the stairs; it is when he hurtles down again, jumping the last three steps and skidding on the hall floor, that the damage is done. Also do not let him jump out of the back of your car. Until he is fully developed just ease him down gently so that there is no shock to his legs when he lands. None of this is intended to suggest that you should mollycoddle your puppy. We believe in free exercise and allow rough and tumble games and are convinced that these help to produce an adult healthy in body and mind.

Ill health in your dog may mean a visit to your vet. Selecting a suitable veterinary surgeon for your Rottweiler is not just a question of looking one up in the telephone directory or going to the nearest. Many breeders take more trouble to find a satisfactory vet than they do to select their own doctor. The relationship between the veterinary profession and the breed has become a little strained over the years. While some of this may be laid at the door of the Rottweiler, most of it stems from human failure and lack of understanding by both vets and Rott owners. Vets are busy people, the cost of equipping and running a practice is high and, as most vets will tell you, their livelihood lies in their hands. If a vet gets badly bitten it can prevent him working for a considerable time. His ideal dog is one that suffers all sorts of undignified and possibly painful investigations without taking exception. The Rottweiler, who is inclined to take the greatest exception to such treatment, does not fit into the pattern. Many members of the profession are arriving in general practice having been told during training that the Rottweiler is dangerous. This has a cumulative effect resulting in the vet approaching the dog giving off emanations of fear; the Rott senses the fear and responds to it, thus confirming the vet's opinion.

We have one basic rule which we insist on with all vets who deal with our dogs. As long as the dog is conscious, one of us remains with him, holding him as required, talking to him and giving him the confidence which comes from knowing that his owner is present and giving the orders. As we always say, 'If anyone is going to be bitten it will be us.' As a result no vet has ever been bitten by one of our Rotts and neither have we. A couple of examples illustrate the point. Roisterer broke a small bone in his toe. It required surgery to open up the toe and sort it out. We did this with a local anaesthetic only. He was up on the operating table, his leg stretched out in front of him with one of us holding him around the neck. He peered at his opened up toe and with a 'sorry but I can't look' expression on his face, turned and tucked his head under one of our arms. The second occasion concerned a three-year-old dog whom we thought had a hairline fracture of a hind leg. With our vet we spent a Sunday lunch time trying to X-ray the leg without using a general anaesthetic. When we tried to turn him on the table to get his leg in position it obviously hurt him. His total reaction was to take one of our hands in his mouth and squeeze. You could never call it a bite but he was showing us that what we were doing hurt him and would we please stop.

Sort out a suitable vet before you need him. It is no use trying to find out whether he is satisfactory when you have an emergency on your hands. Ask whether he is willing to treat your Rottweilers, find out whether he is willing to discuss problems and listen to your suggestions. Experienced dog breeders frequently know more about the health of their dogs than a vet. Blind acceptance by a compliant owner of a vet's first diagnosis may lead to incorrect treatment. Is he a one man band? If his off-duty periods are covered by a locum then you may be chasing all over the countryside at two o'clock in the morning only to finish up with a stand-by vet who cannot cope with Rotts. Is he willing to make house calls at any hour of the day or night? One hears horrific stories of owners ringing their vet in the middle of the night because their bitch is in trouble whelping, only to be told, 'Bring her down to the surgery at 9 o'clock in the morning.' Our own vets have always appreciated that a call from us is urgent and have responded as quickly as possible. There are many practices in almost all areas. Vets are competitive and you pay the bills. If you do not get the service you require go somewhere else.

Do not expect your vet to allow you to be present when your dog is unconscious during a major operation. He will have enough problems without having to pick you up off the floor because you have fainted at the sight of blood.

If you find a vet who fits all these requirements, make a friend of him, pay his bills on time and hang on to him. His help will be invaluable to you. Finally make sure that you, as the owner, can handle your Rottweiler under all circumstances. You can hardly expect the vet to cope if you are frightened to do so. In our experience far too many

Rottweiler owners are afraid, or at least apprehensive, of their own dogs. There should be between you a bond of mutual confidence which allows your Rott to trust you and realize that what is being done is for his benefit.

Prevention is better than cure. A dog that is kept clean, given regular exercise, a warm dry bed and a suitable diet will stand a far better chance of resisting disease than one that lacks these attentions.

Cleanliness starts with the provision of a clean bed. The dog who lives in the house will probably be given his own blanket, which should be contained within some sort of sleeping box or bed. The best beds in our opinion are the fibreglass oval shaped ones available from any pet shop. They are light and easily kept clean. Do, however, make sure that you have one that is large enough for your dog when fully grown. House dogs frequently decide that their bed is an armchair or sofa. If you are willing to allow this there is no objection, but it is sensible that wherever the dog sleeps he knows that this is his bed. He will go to it when told and use it to store his treasures such as an old bone and your socks.

The first requirement for a dog living outdoors is an adequate kennel. Rottweilers are not usually destructive but if they decide to leave home they will quickly break out of a flimsy building. We prefer kennels built of insulated concrete blocks which are strong, reasonably cheap to construct and can be made warm and draught proof. Remember that heat is lost through the roof as well as the walls so that if you use, as you probably will, corrugated roofing sheet, it will require some sort of insulating layer. The ideal layout is a fairly large sleeping area, large enough to contain the sleeping box plus room for the dog to get out of the box to stretch his legs and relieve himself. We do not attempt to train dogs that are in outside kennels to be kennel clean. Remember that they may spend something like 12 hours shut in this area during the winter so they do require plenty of space. The sleeping area will also require ventilation which is best provided by air bricks set high in the wall. Provision must be made in the sleeping area for water containers. We find that a bored Rottweiler will pick up loose water containers, pour the water all over the floor and bash the container against the wall until it is scrap metal. The bucket holders consisting of a metal ring fastened to the wall, which look very professional when first installed, do not work. Our Rottweilers not only removed the bucket but the ring as well. We now use open-topped brick boxes an inch or so higher than the bucket, built into a corner of the kennel. They are made so that the bucket drops inside the box as a close fit. If you use this system make sure you provide drainage holes at the bottom of the box so that water slopped out of the bucket does not accumulate at the bottom.

We build our kennels high enough for a normal human being to stand upright. We do not like having to creep around bent double when cleaning out. We also like our kennels to be large enough for at least two Rotts, for company and mutual warmth.

It is useful if each kennel has electric light and provision for heating. Heating in our adult kennels is provided by metal tubular heaters of the type designed for outdoor use. Ideally these heaters can be mounted within the actual sleeping box protected by a heavy metal grille. Make sure that all electric wiring is adequately protected. Electricians are not always aware of the ability of Rottweilers to pull wiring away from its mounting even when protected by metal conduits.

Each kennel should have its own individual run attached, about 12 ft by 8 ft in size. These in turn can open into your large exercising paddock. We build our runs of concrete blocks to a height of about 4 ft. Above this, to a total height of at least 6 ft, is heavy gauge weldmesh on concrete or metal posts. Chain link fencing, while satisfactory for large runs, is useless for the smaller runs. Rottweilers rapidly reduce it to a tangle of wire. If you are building a range of kennels we find that the 4 ft solid block walls between each run prevents the dogs fighting through the wire but encourages them to stand on their hind legs and even jump. Useful exercise for dogs kept in kennels.

All gates and doors should be metal with strong bolts. Remember that the gates will have to resist pressure from a dog on the inside and also from another dog on the outside, hurling himself at it with the intention of getting at the dog inside.

Kennel sleeping boxes should be covered, with a small draught proof entrance so that the dogs conserve the warmth that they generate. We find the best bedding in kennels to be shredded newspaper which can be bought by the bale. It allows the dog to dig a nest in it, is relatively cheap and can be easily disposed of by burning. Hay or straw are inclined to harbour insects and break down quickly into dust which irritates the dog's eyes and gets into the coat. Rottweilers are quite happy in cold weather but do not like excessive heat. During the summer they will often prefer to be on a cool patch of concrete rather than in their bed. During hot weather it is essential that kennel runs should have plenty of shade and a good airflow.

One final plea for the Rottweiler kept in kennels. He is a sociable chap and likes human companionship. Try and bring him into the house as much as you can or if this is not possible then spend time in the kennel with him. Make his exercise in the big paddock a time when you talk to and play with him.

The quality of a Rottweiler coat is more a matter of correct diet than of grooming. All the same, your Rott does need to be groomed and we find that the preliminary grooming is best done with a wire grooming brush applied gently. These brushes can easily scratch the skin. The wire brush will remove dead hair very efficiently. Follow this with either a rubber grooming glove or a fairly hard bristle brush and give the coat a final polish with a soft cloth or better still a silk scarf. Unlike heavily coated breeds Rottweilers rarely require bathing. If you do need to do so, and you may if your Rott gets a flea or other insect infestation, then we do not recommend that you try and get him in the family bath. We use an ordinary hair spray sprinkler of the kind you may use for washing your own hair. Attached to both the hot and cold taps the spray is taken out of the window so that you can give your dog a shower outside. Pick a warm day for it and make sure you towel him dry. If necessary use an insecticidal shampoo from your vet.

Exercise for the growing puppy we dealt with in Chapter 4, 'Your Rottweiler Puppy'. For the adult dog exercise is dependent on your circumstances, the age of the dog and to a certain extent his own inclinations. Rottweilers, like humans, vary in the amount of exercise they consider necessary. Two or more Rottweilers with access to a fair-sized paddock will exercise each other. However, this does not mean that you can forego walking on a lead which the dog requires both as a discipline and as part of the socialization process. If you like long walks then your Rott is the ideal companion. We would remind you that if you live in an urban area, the Rottweiler, particularly the male, is not the sort of dog you can let loose in the park. At least not until you are satisfied that you have him under perfect control. A good rule is never to let your Rott off the lead unless you can see round the corner. Living in a moderate-sized suburban garden, provided it is well fenced, your Rott will probably get most of the exercise that he needs tearing up and down making sure that the neighbour's cat and the local sparrows do not trespass on his territory. This, plus a trip on the lead down to the shops or the local pub, will be adequate. One thing you cannot do with a Rott is to keep him tied up on a chain in the back yard. He is far too intelligent for this kind of treatment.

Feeding your adult Rottweiler is a question of getting the correct diet combined with what is convenient for you. Most Rottweilers are 'dustbins' and will eat anything that is put before them. They are excellent converters and will thrive on a wide variety of diets. For our dogs living in kennels we feed a maintenance diet of one meal per day. This meal is given in the evening because we believe that they should go to bed on a full stomach, helping them to get a good night's rest. The Rotts living in the house are fed at the same time but are of course let outside last thing at night and in the early morning. In addition to the main meal they all get a snack of hard biscuits in the morning. Dogs who require additional feeding such as stud dogs, in-whelp and lactating bitches and youngsters up to the age of eighteen months receive a second main meal in the morning. Each of our dogs is fed from his own dish and separately from the others. The actual content and quantity of each meal varies for each dog and there is absolute uproar if someone feeds a dog the wrong dinner. Rottweilers vary in their degree of greed. Some will clear their dish in seconds, others prefer to take their time. Separate feeding prevents the slow eater from having his dinner stolen. The basic meal consists of meat, usually tripe and beef, mixed with biscuit. The biscuit element may be a wholemeal biscuit, or one of the complete diets which are available, or both mixed on a half-and-half basis. Whatever biscuit mixture is used it is always soaked with hot water or gravy for an hour or so before feeding. We do not feed the mixture dry as we feel it could cause bloat, an illness we have never had in the kennels. The meat and biscuit mixtures are fed together, not separately, as we find that this encourages the dogs to eat a good quantity of biscuit. We consider that Rottweilers require a fairly high percentage of carbohydrate in their diet. We are not averse to using one of the better quality tinned dog meats as an occasional alternative both as a change and for their convenience factor. A few tins in the car when one is away at a show are a lot easier than bags of smelly tripe.

We do not like what are called 'complete diets' used as such. Apart from the utter boredom for the dog of eating the same thing every day and in spite of the manufacturers' claims, we do not consider that these products, excellent as they may be, provide a satisfactory diet year in and year out. Furthermore in spite of the impressive analysis of protein, carbohydrates etc. listed on the bag, you must be aware that the protein source can be either vegetable, animal or even artificial, manufactured by a chemical process. Some people claim to find them very satisfactory. We prefer to use them as only part of our diet. The animal nutrition experts employed by the manufacturers will of course say that by mixing other foods in with their product we are destroying their carefully created balanced diet. We can only reply that we have been producing fit, healthy, high quality dogs for a lot longer than they have been producing their diets.

There is no reason why you should not use household scraps in your dog's diet. Into our 'dog bowl' goes anything edible that we have not eaten ourselves. This includes surplus greenstuff, root vegetables, leftover potatoes and bread.

Although he is the exception, you will occasionally find a Rottweiler who is a finicky feeder. He is usually the one you are grooming for stardom in the show ring. Competition for the food with another dog is the first possible cure for this. Feed them side by side but hold back the greedy one so that the finicky one is encouraged to eat out of jealousy. If this fails try different foods, fish, eggs, liver, cheese and an excellent one, breast of mutton.

Coat condition can be improved by the addition of a small amount of margarine, vegetable oil or one of the proprietary vitamin E oils. Vitamin and mineral supplements must be treated with care. The dog does not necessarily excrete any surplus and over-enthusiastic use of supplements can cause permanent damage. We have used sterilized bone flour for a long time as a safe form of calcium and it is in fact almost the only supplement we use. S.A.37 and Canovel are popular with many breeders and are used by us for nursing and in-whelp bitches.

7

The Show Ring – Exhibiting

There is no doubt that the most popular dog sport is the beauty show. It attracts far more competitors than any of the working activities and is the aspect of dogs which arouses the interest of the general public. Most people, whether or not interested in dogs, have heard of Crufts and many have visited the show. Beauty shows also, probably unfairly, get the major part of the media coverage. What the non-dog public do not realize is that Crufts is only one out of a total of about 3000 beauty shows, of all types, held throughout the country during the year. These shows include small local shows, larger 'open' shows, breed specialist shows and major 'all breed' championship shows. It is no exaggeration to say that you can, if you wish, go to a dog show at least once every week of the year, the majority of these without travelling enormous distances. At the time of writing there are well over thirty shows per year at which challenge certificates are on offer for Rottweilers.

For the benefit of those not familiar with the structure of the British dog show world we should explain that the Kennel Club licenses shows at a number of different levels. At the bottom of the list, but by no means the least pleasant, are exemption shows.

These gain their name from the fact that they are exempt from most of the Kennel Club regulations governing the holding of shows. They are normally held for the raising of money for a charitable purpose and are restricted to four classes of pedigree dogs. No separate classes for particular breeds may be held and the schedule will usually include a number of fun classes such as 'dog looking most like its owner' or 'dog the judge would most like to take home'. Winning at one of these shows will not hit the headlines in the dog papers, but you may get your picture in your local paper. You will find that a number of these shows are held in your area, especially in the summer months, often in conjunction with a local fête or other event. They are good for beginners, both human and canine, to make a start in the show game. Many experienced exhibitors use them for bringing out young puppies and getting them accustomed to the show ring. Even if you do not win you will have fun and meet other dog enthusiasts.

The next group consists of what are called Limited, Sanction and Primary shows. Again you will find many of these in your area, probably run by local canine societies, although some may be run by Rottweiler breed clubs. The fundamental purpose of these shows is to give a chance of winning to the puppies, youngsters and others by excluding those dogs who have already won the higher awards. In other words a chance for the beginner.

The third type of show is the Open show. This is quite simply what it implies: open to all. Open shows vary in size from being quite small, with only a couple of hundred dogs, to massive affairs approaching the size of some championship shows. Entry in these shows means that you will be up against more competition, possibly including champions, but the classes are still graded in such a way that the lesser qualified dog still has a chance of collecting a prize.

The summit of the show world is the championship show. These are shows at which Kennel Club challenge certificates are on offer for all, or almost all, of the breeds scheduled at the show.

The making of a champion in Britain requires the award to the dog of three challenge certificates by three different championship show judges. Each of these judges signs the certificate to the effect that the judge considers the dog to be worthy of the title of champion. On the day, the dog will have beaten all other dogs of the same sex and breed that are present, including possibly dogs which are already champions. The issue of challenge certificates is controlled by the Kennel Club and only one pair, dog and bitch, is available at each designated show. As we have said, there are over thirty sets of C.C.s issued for Rottweilers each year, the number made available being based on the level of entries of Rottweilers at shows during the preceding years.

It is important to understand that a dog may continue to win C.C.s beyond the three required to give him his title. This means that one outstanding dog may win a large percentage of the C.C.s on offer, thus preventing other dogs achieving their title. While some exhibitors, hungry for champions, may complain that the system prevents them from making their dog into a champion, the system ensures that British champions are of a high quality. As the saying goes, 'If you do not like a particular dog winning all the tickets, then produce a better one to beat it.'

Apart from the general championship shows offering C.C.s for a large number of breeds, there are the breed championship shows, run by breed clubs. These are restricted to the one breed. It is at the Rottweiler breed championship shows that you will see the largest number of high quality Rotts, and the award of the C.C. at such a show carries very considerable prestige.

There are other beauty show activities worthy of your support. Both breed clubs, and general canine societies, run matches. These are normally held in the evening or at weekends and are based on a knock-out system whereby dogs are paired, one is chosen by the judge as the winner and goes on to compete, in subsequent pairs, until it is either beaten or wins 'best in match'. Matches are a great opportunity to try out your youngster, and for both you and the dog to gain experience.

If you do decide that the show game is for you, then one of your first actions should be to join at least one of the Rottweiler breed clubs, and also your local canine society. Membership of these clubs will give you an insight into the show world, the opportunity to decide whether you like it, a lot of helpful advice from more experienced exhibitors and the chance to make many friends.

In the ring at a dog show there are three separate categories of human participants, the exhibitors, the stewards and the judge. We propose to deal mainly with the first and the last. We would hope that you intend to spend a long time in the first category before aspiring to the third. We will deal later with the qualities required in a judge. Firstly, let us discuss those desirable in an exhibitor.

If you are both serious and conscientious about the breeding and showing of dogs, then your first interest should be in the welfare of your chosen breed. In Rottweilers you have chosen a fascinating breed, with a notable past and, we hope, a great future. To the serious breeder the show ring is a means of measuring your success, or failure, as a breeder. You take your dog into the ring in the hope that the quality you consider it has will be confirmed by a knowledgeable judge. The winning of a prize card, or challenge certificate, is merely the documentary proof of the dog's excellence. A win with a poor quality dog, over dogs which are better than yours, should not be a source of gratification but a reason for criticizing the judge's ability. Regrettaby some exhibitors today are more interested in the prize cards than the dogs. We hope that you will not be one of these and that you will admire, and applaud, a win by a rival's dog because you can appreciate his quality. Kennel blindness, which is the inability to see good in any dog other than your own, is probably the most common affliction in the show ring today.

Many first-time exhibitors, certain that their dog is the greatest in the world, are not merely disappointed when they find out that he is not, they are convinced that the whole thing is a 'closed shop', and that all the top awards go to those who are famous breeders and probably judges as well. The statement that the majority of the top awards go to the top breeders is true. Not because they are top breeders, but because they breed the best stock, which makes them top breeders. It is also true that the best dogs usually win. Proof of this can be seen in the occasional dog, bred or exhibited, by a newcomer to the show ring, which repeatedly beats the old hands. Finally, if you think about it, all those who are now at the top had to start at the bottom, and reached their present position by sheer hard work, ability and perseverance.

There are no easy short cuts. Money can buy you a top quality Rottweiler and provided you do not make too great a mess of handling him, you will win with him. Money will not, however, buy you the ability to use that dog for breeding and so breed another good one. Expensive advertisements extolling the quality of your dogs may create an impression of success. They will not win you the respect of dog people as a knowledgeable and esteemed breeder. Of course, if you really have a lot of money you can employ a knowledgeable kennel manager, or manageress, to do it all for you. This may very well create a famous kennel, but at the end of the day, it will be the manager who is the famous dog person, not you.

While we hope, for your sake, that your first Rottweiler is an absolute flyer and brings you enormous success in the ring, it will be better for your soul, and for your future, if you have to struggle to succeed. Instant success brings the belief that the whole thing is easy, with a nasty let down when you subsequently discover that it is not always so. Alternatively, your quick rise to the top may convince you that you are much better at the game than all the other people who have to struggle and learn the hard way. This might be good for your ego but it will not make you a dog expert.

If you are wise you will have visited a number of shows as a spectator. You will have watched what happens and how experienced exhibitors show their dogs. Many exhibitors find their first entry into the ring embarrassing, and are far more worried about looking foolish themselves than about making a good job of handling their exhibit. The best way to call attention to yourself is to give an impression of utter incompetence. Both judge and spectators are interested in the dog, not you, so forget about your appearance or whether you sound absurd talking baby-talk to your Rott, and get on with the job of showing him. Showing a dog successfully is a combination of the quality of the dog and the ability of the handler to show him to his best advantage.

In order to avoid looking a fool in the ring you need to know the procedure, and to have trained your dog to comply with it. Judges can, within certain limits, judge by any method they choose, but most of them will stick fairly closely to the accepted routine. At the start, all the exhibitors will be lined up by the steward along the side of the ring. Each exhibitor will wear a ring number which will either have been placed in advance on your bench, or have been given to you by the steward when you entered the ring. Have a safety pin, or better still a proper number clip ready, so that you can pin on your number. Do not tuck the number in your pocket, or promptly drop it, so that you have to chase it around the ring. The ring number is the only means that the judge has of identifying your dog when he is examining him, or placing him. It will not please the judge if he cannot see it easily. Also make sure that you are wearing the right number. It causes utter confusion if you win wearing the number of another dog. Incidentally, only old professional terrier handlers wear felt hats with the number tucked into the band. When you line up in the ring the steward may issue the instruction 'old dogs on that side'. This does not mean that he is sorting out the geriatric pensioners. It is the term used to describe dogs which have already been examined by the judge in a previous class. Also, when the judge or steward tells you to move to a particular spot, stay there. Do not wander off somewhere else because you wish to talk to a friend at the ringside.

Having got you all lined up, the judge will probably take a slow stroll along the line in order to get a general impression of the class. While he does this your dog should be standing quietly, all four feet on the ground looking his best. First impressions count. At all times, while in the ring, you should have one eye on your dog to see that he is standing correctly, and the other on the judge, ready to receive his instructions. Judges do not like having to come across the ring in order to attract your attention and tell you to take first place.

The judge will then examine each dog individually by calling you, one at a time, into the middle of the ring. He wants to be able to see your dog standing quietly while he moves around him assessing him from all angles. He may wish to touch him to check for construction and for coat quality. If the dog is a male he will wish to check that he is entire, a slightly undignified procedure which your Rott may resent and must be trained to accept. While the judge is making the overall examination your dog should remain facing the same way. It is no help to the judge if, after looking at his head, he moves around to look at the other end and the dog turns to face him again. Judges need to see a Rott's head in considerable detail. Train your dog to stand so that the judge can get a clear view of the head. It is not unusual for the dog to be stood so that his nose is practically touching the handler. The judge finds himself behind the handler, peering over his shoulder, or under his arm.

You will be asked how old your dog is. Make sure that you know the answer, but it does not have to be an exact statement of year, months and days.

You will be asked to show the judge your dog's teeth. The usual request is, 'May I see the bite?' Do not, as many newcomers do, reply, 'He doesn't bite, he's as good as a lamb.' Some judges will pull back the lips themselves. Apart from increasing the risk of being bitten, it is unhygienic for the judge to go from one mouth to another, with the risk of transferring infection. You should learn to show the teeth yourself, and tell the judge you will do so. He will wish to see how the front teeth are set and also check on the pre-molars. When he is looking at the front teeth he is interested in whether the dog has, or has not, got the correct scissor bite. He requires the mouth to be closed for this, not opened wide as if for a visit to the dentist. Just pull back the lips in the front and then the flews at each side.

Having examined your dog the judge will then ask you to move him. The usual request is for you to move in a triangle. This enables the judge to see the dog's hind action as the dog moves away from him, his gait from the side as you move across the ring, and his front movement as you return. When you start your return leg of the triangle see where the judge is standing and aim for him. He wants to see the dog's action as he comes towards him and cannot do so if you veer off to some other corner of the ring. When you move, there will be other dogs standing at the side of the ring. Try and carry out your triangle without charging full tilt into another dog. The judge may then ask you to move once more, 'straight up and down'. In other words, straight away from him to the end of the ring, and straight back again. At the end of moving your dog it is usual to 'set your dog up' in the standing position in front of the judge, for him to have a final look at him. He will then ask you to return to your place at the side of the ring. Stay in the same order at the side of the ring. Do not wander off to some other position. The judge is working his way through the dogs in sequence and you will not be popular if you get out of order. While the judge is examining the other dogs in the class – he may have twenty or thirty to do – you can allow your Rott to relax, sit or lie down, or even have a cuddle. Do not try and keep him standing in a show stance during this time. By the time you need him to stand up again he will be bored stiff.

Some judges will, after examining every dog in the class, require all the exhibits to 'gait' around the ring together. Unless the judge is trying to impress the ringside with his knowledge of Rottweiler judging in Germany, this gaiting will only consist of two or three circuits. Just long enough for him to compare the movement of all the exhibits. With the large Rottweiler entry at shows many judges sensibly restrict this gaiting to their final selection of, perhaps, six or eight dogs.

Make a mental note of the first dog to be examined by the judge so that you will know when he has finished. This is the moment to bring your dog up into his show stance again, and to put all your effort into making him look as perfect as possible. The judge is making his final selection. If he decides to award you a prize he will call you into the centre of the ring, lining you up in 1st, 2nd and 3rd order. Do not relax; keep your dog showing at his best. Judges sometimes make a last minute change at this moment. At last he has entered the ring number in his judging book. The steward will give out the prize cards; the judge will make notes about the dogs. Congratulations, you have won!

All this may seem a long and frightening procedure. It is really very simple. You and your dog have to be able to do three things. Firstly, to behave properly in the ring; secondly, to stand in a show stance while being examined; and thirdly, to move.

Let's take them one at a time. We have already told you the full sequence of events. As far as your own behaviour in the ring is concerned we will talk about that later. As for your dog, you must have him under proper control when showing. While any knowledgeable judge will be aware of, and make allowance for, the Rottweiler character, you cannot take a raving lunatic which you are unable to control into the show ring. Apart from the fact that the judge will be unable to assess the dog if he is continually on his hind legs, roaring defiance at all and sundry, you will be unpopular with other exhibitors and possibly find that you are asked to leave the ring and even banned by the Kennel Club.

Control is a combination of mental domination, establishment of a mutual bond between you and the dog and the simple obedience training we have already discussed.

You have, we hope, been training your puppy to stand from an early age, using the 'bait' method. The majority of Rottweilers will show well for this combination of greed and anticipation. This training should continue right through the dog's show life even if it is only for a few seconds in the kitchen when he is made to stand for a biscuit. Some Rotts, particularly males, are too interested in what is going on around them to bother with food in the ring. Experiment with different methods of standing, and if your Rott will stand without food, by all means let him do so. Not using food does solve the problem of the dog having a mouthful of liver at the moment the judge wishes to see his teeth.

Movement in the show ring should be at the pace which shows your dog off to the best advantage: probably a steady trot for the dog and a slow run for yourself. Find yourself an area in the garden about the size of the average show ring and practise moving in the triangle, straight up and down and gaiting in a circle. You and the dog need to practise together, firstly so that you can adjust your pace to that of the dog, and secondly to avoid both of you falling over each other, particularly on the turns. Remember that the judge is looking at the dog, not you, and make sure that whichever way you turn the dog is on the judge's side of you. The judge cannot see the dog if he is moving on your far side. Occasionally a judge will demand that you walk your dog at a slow pace. We have never seen any benefit in so doing, other than showing the ringside that the judge is different from all the others. Because of his size and build, a Rottweiler moving at a slow walk drops into what can only be described as a waddle. This slow movement certainly does not show the Rott off to his best advantage and, in our opinion, tells the judge nothing at all.

You will need to accustom your Rott to having his teeth looked at. Practise this at home in any spare moment. Use the command 'teeth' or 'mouth', gently pull back the lips or flews as appropriate and give lots of praise when he does not object.

The paper work involved in dog showing is quite simple. Your Rottweiler should have been registered at the Kennel

Club and, if you did not breed him, you will have received a transfer form which you should complete, so that the dog is registered in your name.

You can obtain a schedule for your chosen show by a telephone call to its secretary. This will include an entry form, details of all the classes and other information. Complete the entry form very carefully and send it together with the entry fee by the closing date given in the schedule.

Having dealt with the paper work you have a few weeks to get your Rott ready for the show. Continue to practise all the show training we have outlined. A daily brushing is the only basic preparation you need with this breed, and a well-fed puppy will have a naturally glossy coat. Unless he rolls in something objectionable the day before the show, do not bath him, as this spoils the texture of the coat. The few long hairs on the tail should be trimmed off and further trimming is unnecessary, although some people like to neaten the hairs at the back of the hind legs.

On the day of the show, make sure you have with you: exhibitor's pass and car park label, a bag containing a water bowl and bottle of water, grooming things, benching equipment, his blanket for the bench and titbits if necessary. Having arrived at the show in good time so that neither you nor the dog is flustered, look for your bench and settle your dog comfortably and attach him to the ring provided. A benching chain is recommended as the safest, but because this makes a great deal of noise rattling against the metal sides of the bench, and this could be frightening for the pup at his first show, it may be preferable to use a leather leash, which must be short enough to prevent him jumping off the bench. A puppy that is not used to being restricted may well try to get off the bench, and for this reason, a choke chain should never be used, as there is a danger of choking or discomfort, and therefore a leather collar is advisable. After settling him comfortably on the bench, do not immediately go away and leave him, but give him time to get used to the strange and noisy surroundings. If you do have to leave him, ask a neighbouring exhibitor to keep an eye on him for a few minutes. It cannot be stressed too strongly that your dog's first show should be a happy experience.

Next, buy a catalogue to check your classes and ring

number. Find out where the ring is and, if possible, the approximate time of judging. Then try to relax before you are called into the ring.

If you are showing a puppy at his first show, it is far more important that it should be an enjoyable occasion for him than that you should win. Remember that everything will be strange, exciting and perhaps a little frightening. Even if you both make a mess of it, you still hope that your dog has a long show career in front of him, so do not upset him and create a dislike of shows at this his first attempt. Dog showing is a serious business but do not take it too seriously at first.

As an exhibitor you should consider your own appearance as well as that of your Rott. Whether male or female the theme should be sensible, practical and comfortable. We have already said that it is the dog who is on exhibition, not you. It is not an occasion for wearing your latest expensive outfit, especially as you may be more interested in preserving your clothes rather than showing the dog. Avoid long coats which flap around the dog's head and large unusual hats which upset him. For the lady handler miniskirts and low necklines may have some effect on a few male judges, but the reputation you are likely to acquire will not necessarily be that of an expert dog handler. High heels are also most unsuitable for showing a Rottweiler.

Even if it is obvious to you and everybody else at the ringside that the judge is crooked, hopelessly incompetent and blind, you should not allow your feelings to become known while in the ring or even in its vicinity. The Kennel Club quite rightly believes that judges should be protected from such attacks while officiating. Your redress is not to show under that judge on a subsequent occasion, or to make your dissatisfaction known via your breed club and the show organizers. Bear in mind that the judge's opinion of your dog may not, quite rightly, agree with your own and that out of some thirty dogs in a class, only the two or three winners will be entirely satisfied with the awards given.

Under Kennel Club regulations, it is possible for you to raise an objection if you consider that you have suffered unfairly by the action of another person who had, like yourself, submitted to Kennel Club jurisdiction by registering a dog and entering at a show. While we would never suggest that people who deliberately break the rules should be allowed to escape unpunished, we would advise you to think carefully before rushing to the show secretary waving the rule book. Many so-called misdemeanours are errors rather than deliberately improper actions. It does not make your dog any better in the eyes of the judge if, having been placed second, you succeed in getting the first prize winner disqualified because of some minor and unintentional error by the exhibitor, the steward, or more rarely, the judge. Barrack room lawyers are not popular in the dog game.

Dog showing can be a wonderful and rewarding sport giving you many years of enjoyment and interest. In a few cases it can bring you fame within the not insignificant world of dogs. Even if it does not, you will be actively involved with Rottweilers and what more can you ask than that?

8

The Show Ring – Judging

Many exhibitors eventually decide that they would like to judge their breed or even a number of breeds. We should explain that there are two categories of judges, the variety judge, often called an 'all-rounder', and the breed judge. In theory, the all-rounder has such an extensive knowledge of dogs of virtually all breeds that he is able to judge any of them. Quite a number of all-rounder judges believe this to be true, certainly as far as they themselves are concerned if not of all the others. There was a time when the best of the all-rounders, probably someone who had started as kennel staff and progressed to kennel management or professional handling, did have the depth of knowledge which made his opinion of value to all breeds. Sadly there are few of them left. A small number without this background have raised themselves, by hard work and dedication, to a standard of ability which is acknowledged throughout the world. Sadly again, they are few in number. The saying used to be that the all-rounder kept the breed sound, while the breed specialist dealt with breed points. Today it is certainly true to say that the best breed specialists are as knowledgeable about general soundness as the all-rounder and certainly know more about their chosen breed.

Within the confines of this book we are only concerned with the subject of acting as a Rottweiler breed specialist judge. Quite enough for anyone to start off with.

Anyone aspiring to become a Rottweiler breed judge should set himself a number of goals to achieve before accepting an appointment. These are: a reasonable knowledge of the way a dog is constructed, a detailed knowledge of the Rottweiler standard of breed points and their correct inter-pretation, and the ability to apply this knowledge in the ring. To these we must add the need to control and organize the judging of a class in the show ring, and a very desirable ability which is the dog equivalent of the gardener's green fingers. An instinctive grasp of what makes a dog good or bad. The final requirement is confidence in oneself. Regrettably there are many judges who have this last requirement but are sadly lacking in the former ones. These qualifications may appear to be quite simple and easily learnt in a matter of a few months or in perhaps a year or so. Far from being a simple task undertaken lightly, we would suggest that the ability to judge Rottweilers or, for that matter, any other breed, is something which takes many years of hard work and practical experience.

The best qualification for judging is that over a considerable number of years you have bred stock with which you have consistently won in the show ring. By this we mean that you have made the breeding decisions, whelped and reared the puppies, selected the ones that you considered to be the best and proved your competence by their success in the ring. In short you can evaluate the ability of a judge by the stock he himself shows. There was a time when responsible breeders did not consider themselves qualified to judge at any level until they had both bred and made up a champion. Circumstances today mean that this standard of excellence is no longer possible but it is still a worthwhile aim. The mere fact that you have bought a Rottweiler and shown him successfully is not sufficient; neither are many years of unsuccessful showing and/or breeding. It is not a good reason for you to judge because Mrs A or Mr B is judging and therefore why shouldn't you. Neither should it be approached on the basis that if you judge you will gain benefit as an exhibitor. This last reason can be counter-productive, as you will probably upset many exhibitors who are also judges. Please, therefore, do not hurry into judging. Satisfy yourself that you are really competent and have something to offer the breed before you rush into the middle of the ring.

Assuming that you are a successful breeder and exhibitor, what further step can you take to improve your knowledge? Acting as a ring steward is one. This gives you the opportunity to study the entries in some detail and, if the judge is agreeable, to learn his or her opinion of them. Stewarding will also give you experience of ring control. Most shows are happy to accept volunteer stewards, and if you approach breed judges they may be prepared to take you as their steward. Remember that the judge will be busy and concentrating on his job. Save any long discussion you may wish to have for the lunch break or the end of the day.

Many breed clubs run courses to train judges. These vary in quality and are not really a substitute for the type of experience we have suggested is necessary. Attendance at one of these courses is worthwhile in order to gain additional knowledge, but a 'pass' at the end of the course should not be considered as automatically qualifying you as a breed judge.

Having reached a reasonable level of competence how do you get a judging appointment? A suitable first appointment would be four classes at a show scheduling a number of different breeds. Such shows are usually looking for judges in their local area, and if you have achieved some small reputation as a successful exhibitor you will probably be asked if you are willing to judge. It is accepted that such shows are where new judges learn their trade. Do not pester show secretaries with requests for judging appointments or even, as has been done, send out a 'mailing shot' giving details of all your successes and suggesting that you be allowed to judge. Such letters, quite rightly, usually go straight into the waste paper basket. Be patient the longer you wait the more you should know when you do judge. Wait until you are asked.

When you are asked to judge the secretary will probably enquire about expenses and fees. Few breed judges demand a fee and in our opinion should be happy to judge without one. It is, after all, an honour that exhibitors are prepared to seek your opinion of their Rottweiler. Expenses, which are basically travelling costs, are another matter. With the possible exception of breed club shows we consider that all judges should be entitled to their out-of-pocket expenses. In fact we will go further and suggest that such payments should be made compulsory under Kennel Club regulations. There is one very good reason for this. Many people who would make excellent judges are prevented from doing so because of the cost involved. Others of much lesser ability, who are willing to offer their services for nothing, often obtain appointments for this reason alone. It is totally unfair that shows should be bribed into accepting those judges who can afford to pay their own expenses.

Now let's get you into the ring judging Rottweilers. It is courteous to your exhibitors to dress appropriately. A tee shirt and jeans may be sensible for an exhibitor but not for the judge. Do not wear floppy garments which get in the way of either yourself or the dogs. Be prepared for the vagaries of the weather. You may be judging indoors or outside, in hot sunshine, cold winds or rain. Please arrive in plenty of time. Not only must you not keep your exhibitors waiting, but the show will offer you a cup of coffee on arrival and you will need time to settle down after your journey and to meet your steward.

As an exhibitor you are already familiar with the normal ring procedure. When you come to make your individual examination we suggest that you always work in a predetermined sequence. Ask the age as soon as the exhibit is brought to you. You can then bear it in mind as you carry out your examination. Secondly, examine the teeth and bite before the handler has gone to all the trouble to get the dog standing in a show stance. All too often the dog is carefully placed by his handler and all his efforts are wasted when the judge, having waited until the dog is standing, asks to see the bite. Get this over first and then allow the handler to stand his dog. Be patient with the first time exhibitor and with the young puppy. You too were once a beginner and we hope that you had to solve the problems of showing a puppy on its first time in the ring. Rough treatment of either handler or puppy can mean that both are lost to the show ring in the future. Also, there is nothing heroic about insisting on seeing the teeth of a fully grown male Rott who is making it very clear that someone will get bitten if you persist. If you do get one like this it is far better to leave him quietly out of your final placings rather than make a great fuss about sending him out of the ring as being vicious.

There is no requirement for you to assess the temperament of the Rottweilers before you. Equally there is no rule that says you should not. If you do decide to test temperament make sure that it is consistent for all the dogs entered. Do not, as we have seen done, deliberately try and provoke a known aggressive dog in the hope that you will be given the excuse to send him out of the ring. Neither do we respect the judge who deliberately sets out to upset an apprehensive youngster so that he can then pontificate on poor temperament.

Still on the subject of your actions in the ring, we would suggest that your first judging appointment is not the occasion for introducing your own new-fangled ideas as to how judging should be carried out. It may be surprising, but it is not unknown for a first-time judge to approach his task with the intention of showing everybody else how it should be done. Leave it until you have had years of experience and preferably do not even do it then.

As a short-coated breed, the Rottweiler's construction should be clearly visible to you without excessive handling. Apart from checking coat-texture, undercoat, entirety and perhaps a touch at the shoulders and hindquarters, it is possible to judge a Rottweiler while standing three feet away from it. All through this book we have urged you to respect the Rott's dignity. Give the same respect when you are judging. You will see judges with an expression of deep concentrated thought, running their hands lovingly over every curve of the dog's body. They are discovering nothing about the dog that cannot be seen with their eyes, and the entire performance is intended to give the impression that they are making a very thorough examination. In fact it normally indicates that they are not at all sure what to do next.

Having examined the dog you will need to move him. A triangle followed by a straight up and down should give you adequate opportunity to see all aspects of his movement. Gaiting the dogs around the ring can give you a further opportunity to compare one dog with another, but beware of the problems of large entries and small rings. Rottweilers are inclined to dislike having another one galloping behind them with their nose a few inches from their rear. If you intend to gait the class it is better left until you are sorting out your final selection.

There is considerable misunderstanding of the reasons for gaiting. In Germany Rotts are gaited around the ring for long periods, often of half an hour or more. This is not done because the judge is unable to assess movement in a shorter period. The intention is to see whether the dog breaks down after prolonged movement. As this must be done within the confines of a show ring, with the dog leaning into the same shoulder all the time we are doubtful whether it is a fair test of endurance and movement. The only fair test, in our opinion, would be to move the dog across country for a mile or so and this is obviously impossible in the show ring. Even if you accept the German method as being a reasonable test of fitness, the time required is totally unacceptable under the conditions applying in the UK show world. We would, therefore, argue that the 'twenty times around the ring' demanded by a few judges is neither sufficient as a test of endurance nor necessary for the judge to assess movement. It becomes nothing more than an attempt to introduce German judging methods without understanding the underlying reasons for them.

The time has come to sort out your placings. With a large class it is reasonable to pull out a final selection of, say, eight dogs, clear the ring of the others and then make your final choice. When you select this group do make it clear that you are not, at this stage, making your final placing. Many an exhibitor has been disappointed at having been pulled out first to find that he is actually eighth.

You are required to place your winners from left to right with the first on the left. There are, of course, a number of different lines running from left to right depending on where you stand in the ring. We suggest you decide which position you are using and stick to it for all classes. Nothing looks more incompetent to the ringside than if the position that was first in one class is very highly commended in the next.

In subsequent classes, after the first, you may have dogs that were judged and placed in a previous class. The steward should, under your guidance, place them at one side of the ring, in order of their wins. Remember, however, that the ultimate responsibility is yours. You cannot blame the steward if in a later class you reverse the placings of winners from a previous class. You can, of course, deliberately reverse placings from an earlier class on the grounds that a dog looks better in this class than he did in his previous one. If you do deliberately reverse then announce this straightaway giving your reasons. No one will believe you if you claim to have done so deliberately when your reversal is pointed out to you at the end of your judging.

Double handling, which is the attraction of the dog by a second person outside the ring, is prohibited under Kennel Club regulations. This is the opposite to what is allowed on the Continent, where the entire family join in to show their dog to his best advantage. We have an open mind as to whether double handling should, or should not, be allowed, but it is quite certain that it is impossible to legislate against a husband who suddenly develops a bad cough at the ringside when his wife is showing their dog. We suggest that, unless it becomes too blatant or appears to interfere with other exhibitors, you should turn a blind eye.

Judging, especially at major shows, places many pressures on the judge. Do not be surprised if, during the few weeks before you judge, you have a sudden rush of puppy enquiries, bookings for your stud dog and even invitations to dinner. Deal with these as you think fit. Most of them will fade away after you have judged. You may look around the ring and say to yourself, 'That is my best friend, that is next week's judge, that one was bred by me, that one is by my stud dog, that one has driven 300 miles to show under me and that one is my worst enemy.' Any attempt to place the dogs taking all these factors into account is courting disaster. There is only one basis on which to make your awards, and that is that you are convinced that your selected prize winners are better Rottweilers than those placed under them. One sometimes hears a judge say that he considered dog 'A' to be the best but could not place him first as he belonged to his best friend. It is just as dishonest to reject the best for this reason as it is to put up a bad one because he is bred by you or owned by a friend. Human nature makes all of us susceptible to these influences. We can only advise you not to fall into the trap of judging 'at the wrong end of the lead'.

By the time you are considered worthy to award challenge certificates you should be an extremely experienced judge. We would only remind you that a C.C. is not merely the best Rottweiler present on the day; it is a declared standard of excellence in that you sign it to the effect that, in your opinion, the dog is worthy of becoming a champion. It is therefore possible, and in fact is required of you, that you should withhold the C.C. if, in your opinion, there is no dog present who reaches this standard. With the present quality of Rottweilers we consider that it is very unlikely that you will have grounds for withholding. We trust that it is obvious to you that if you withhold the C.C. you cannot present the Reserve C.C. as a lesser award, as this also states that the winner is worthy of the C.C. and, therefore, of the title of champion, if the C.C. winner is disqualified.

Judging Rottweilers should be considered by you to be an honour and a way in which you can serve your breed. It is in the show ring that the quality of the stock being produced is assessed, faults and virtues recognized, and the way ahead identified for future progress. While breeders must never lose sight of the temperament and working ability requirements of the Rottweiler, it is the show ring which provides the focal point of the breed's development. A Rottweiler specialist judge carries great responsibility for the breed.

9
Breeding – Whelping and Rearing

The breeding of a litter of Rottweiler puppies is not a task to be undertaken lightly. First let us look at some of the excuses for breeding given by bitch owners. The honest but unacceptable one is that it is a means of making money. It is true that if you have a pet bitch, which you would have even if you did not breed from her, and do not count as debits her purchase price, her rearing and keep, her housing, heating and vet's bills, her keep in her well-earned old age, and your time, then you can if you are lucky expect a profit out of a litter of puppies. Not a large profit, but a profit. However, taking all the costs given above into account, bearing in mind the hourly rate for your work and allowing 'double time' for what the trade unions call 'unsocial hours', your profit will be very small. Furthermore, while we see no reason why people should not make money out of their dogs as a by-product of their interest in and knowledge of them, we find their exploitation purely for profit to be extremely distasteful. One puppy buyer we know, who commented on the undernourished appearance of her purchase, was told that the 'breeders' kept eight bitches purely to produce puppies, which were reared on cat food and rice. The enterprise was explained as providing the means to educate their children privately.

A common excuse, even propounded by vets, is that it will be good for the bitch to have a litter as she will feel deprived if she does not. This is merely being anthropomorphic. While a bitch may be extremely maternal while nursing a litter, she frequently hates the sight of her puppies once they are weaned and certainly does not go through life regretting that she has not had a puppy.

There is only one reason for breeding Rottweiler puppies,

and that is that you believe you have a bitch whose qualities are such that the breed would gain benefit from her off-spring. This does not necessarily mean that you must be certain of producing a litter of champions. It does mean that you hope to produce puppies which will be as good as, or better than, their parents. That you hope to produce at least one who will be of excellent quality, and that all the rest of the litter will be a credit to the breed even if they only fulfil their function by being much loved and sensible companions in a pet home. Even if you fail in this aim, and all of us fail at times, no one will blame you if you have really tried to achieve these objectives.

If you do own a bitch of the required quality there are still questions you must ask yourself. Are you willing to go to the trouble and expense of mating her to the most suitable Rottweiler sire? Have you the facilities for whelping her and rearing the puppies? Can you afford to feed the bitch to a high standard and also the puppies during weaning? Are you certain that prospective buyers are of the same opinion as you as to the puppies' quality? In other words, do you have a market for them? Are you able to 'run on' for some weeks or months any puppy which remains unsold after eight or nine weeks? Do you have the time and the temperament to donate virtually your entire life for a period of some ten weeks to the bitch and her puppies? If the entire adult household goes to work from 9 a.m. to 5 p.m. then this rules you out. It can only be described as criminal to leave a bitch and her puppies unattended for this length of time. Neither is it acceptable during weaning to leave down a dish of food considered sufficient for the day. The puppies will eat some and soil and trample the rest. Finally, after taking all the trouble to rear a good healthy puppy and find him a suitable home, are you willing and able to take that dog back as a puppy or a young adult if, possibly through no fault of the dog or purchasers, they cannot keep him? Rottweiler Welfare and similar rescue societies do not exist to sort out problems which you have helped to create and have made money out of. Regrettably most of the work they do is just this: picking up the pieces after greedy people.

If you can truthfully answer yes to all these questions then you can aspire to calling yourself a Rottweiler breeder with all the responsibilities which the term implies.

Where will your bitch whelp and rear her puppies? When one asks this question owners sometimes look rather vague and then say, 'We have a shed at the bottom of the garden.' Just 'a shed' will not do. The whelping room must be warm, dry and suitable for you as well as the bitch to spend several nights in. While you may be unkind enough to let her spend these nights in a cold, cramped, draughty shed, are you prepared to crouch there with her in a building only 4 ft high? So the first requirement for a whelping room is that it is comfortable not only for the bitch but for yourself. Many people sleep on a camp bed in the whelping room for the few days before and after the whelping. Ideally a room in the house is best. A utility room or a spare bedroom. It should be located in a quiet area away from domestic traffic and visitors. Rottweiler bitches, with their strong guarding instincts, are inclined to leap out of the box scattering puppies in all directions every time the front door bell rings. The walls and floor of the whelping room should be hygienic and easily cleaned. You will require electric light and an electric socket for an overhead heater. It helps also to have some form of background heater such as a radiator. You will need to be able to maintain a room temperature of 60 degrees and a temperature of 75 to 80 degrees over the actual whelping box. To allow for hot weather you will also need adequate and controllable ventilation. These are the basic requirements for the whelping room. A useful improvement is the provision of an inner run within the room so that you can get through the outer door without bitch and puppies pushing past you. It can also provide a useful viewing area for indulging in that most delightful but time-consuming sport of 'puppy watching'. The gate into the inner run should be in two halves. Both top and bottom half should be capable of being opened and closed separately. The bottom half of the gate should be about 16 ins. Low enough for the bitch to jump over and for you to step over but high enough to stop young puppies. The top half of the gate can be as high as you wish, probably the same height as the run, which should be sufficient to keep the bitch in. You will find that this half gate arrangement is invaluable in any pen where puppies are kept. Trying to close a normal door with ten rumbustious Rottweiler youngsters determined to come through it is a task that infuriates the most patient person. With the half gate you simply lift the puppies over the top. With a large litter, or when the puppies begin to grow, it is unkind to keep the bitch permanently shut in with them over long periods. Sharp teeth always tugging at her will allow her no rest. With the top half of the gate open she can jump into the space outside the run for peace and quiet until nature tells her that it is feeding time again.

You will need a whelping box. An old blanket thrown into a corner with no side walls to stop the puppies rolling away will not do. We have tried a number of different designs. For a Rottweiler the totally enclosed box with a top and a small entrance does not work. It is warm and cosy and the bitch feels safe and protected, but because of the need for it to be at least 30 ins high you will find it very difficult to bend over the high sides during all the work you have to do. Over the years we have found nothing better than an open-topped box 3 ft by 4 ft in size with sides about 16 ins high. One side of the box should be open to the floor level with three-inch-wide boards available to drop into grooves at each end. You should have sufficient boards to raise the side to the full height of the other sides. When the bitch is heavy in whelp she will want to get in and out without having to hoist her bulk over the high sides. When she has her puppies you will want to stop them falling out of the box so you raise the height of the side. Bearing in mind that it is a good idea to discard old whelping boxes when they get a bit battered and stained, the cheapest form of construction is heavy external plywood or chipboard. Do not varnish the inside of the box, particularly the floor. Puppies need to be able to get a grip when starting to move about and a smooth floor, which you may think is desirable for cleaning purposes, will not allow this.

So you now have a whelping room, a whelping box and a Rottweiler bitch. You should not breed from her until she is about two years old. Any younger, when she is not fully developed, is unfair to her and creates the risk of producing inferior puppies. Furthermore, she will probably be temperamentally underdeveloped to cope with the responsibility of motherhood. We know of one bitch bred from at fifteen months who considered her puppies to be toys. She happily spent her time tossing them around the box as if they were her ball and rubber ring.

Now comes the choice of a sire. The general dog owning public are inclined to blame all the troubles of their dog on what they call 'inbreeding'. They are not quite sure what it means but feel that it must be something like incest with all that this word implies. There are three possible relationships between your two Rottweiler parents that you can consider. Firstly, an outcross mating. This simply means that dog and bitch are not related; or at least not within the last four generations. The effect of this in layman's language is to throw the characteristics of the two parents into a hat, stir them up and see what comes out. It will produce a wide variation of type within one litter. It can produce the occasional excellent animal. It can also produce some very poor ones. All, as we have said, in the same litter. If you do it again with the next generation you will get the same variation in type. Outcrossing is used in Germany to a very great extent and a number of restrictions are placed on the use of any other breeding method.

The second possible relationship is known as inbreeding, by which we mean the breeding of two closely related animals such as brother/sister, father/daughter, etc. This method requires a lot of knowledge and a lot of care and in general we would not recommend it. It is generally said that Cleopatra was the result of generations of inbreeding and look where she finished up. We ourselves, in another breed, mated brother and sister and produced a champion who still holds the breed record for achieving 22 C.C.s and their descendants still play a major part in the breed today. We should, however, point out that at that time there was literally no other pure-bred stock in the world that we could use.

The third alternative method is to line-breed, which is the mating of two animals which are not too closely related. The classic line-breeding relationship is grandfather/granddaughter, but there are obviously a number of others. Line breeding can be considered to be the method which has helped British dog breeders become predominant throughout the world.

There is one simple rule to remember. Line breeding, and in this context we include inbreeding, fixes the characteristics of the parents in their progeny. If those characteristics are good you will fix good ones; those characteristics which are bad will also become fixed. The more generations you apply the method to, the firmer you will fix these characteristics.

If you wish, you can get yourself involved in the study of genetics. Whether you will be a better dog breeder as a result is doubtful. We can think of one or two dog breeders who are highly qualified geneticists. None of these have shown any signs of breeding better dogs than we ordinary mortals. Even those who write books and articles claiming to explain genetics in simple terms for dog breeders manage to lose most of us in the first few minutes. In Rottweilers we do not have the problems of colour variation stemming from the mating of two animals of different colours. For which, in our opinion, Rottweiler breeders can be thankful.

Let us try to reduce the choice of a sire to a few simple points:

(a)   If the bitch is line-bred and the dog also, then they will tend to pass on their characteristics to their progeny. If only one is line-bred then the characteristics of the line-bred parent will tend to dominate the characteristics of the outcross parent but not entirely. Use the two pedigrees to establish this.

(b)   Look at both of them with a critical eye. You will probably think that your bitch is perfect. To you she may be, but if you can see only her virtues and not her faults, then ask an experienced breeder to tell you honestly what they are. If the breeder turns your swan into an ugly duckling do not fly into a rage and claim that she does not know what she is talking about. If you asked for honest advice be grateful for getting it.

(c)   Look for a male of the highest quality you can find. One who complements the good points of your bitch and does not have her faults. Using a poor quality sire will achieve nothing and result in poor quality puppies being dumped on the market.

(d)   Remember the old dog breeders' saying: 'If you like a dog, use his father.'

Once you have chosen your sire it is sensible to contact his owners. Tell them what you hope to do and ask their opinion. A reputable owner will want to know whether your bitch complies with the criteria we have already given. If everything is agreed the sire's owners will probably ask you to let them know the first day that your bitch comes into season. This is considered to be the first day that she shows a blood-coloured discharge from the vulva. Some bitches produce a copious discharge, much to the detriment of the carpet if they live indoors. Others will keep themselves so clean that you may not notice it. While the textbooks will tell you that a bitch comes into season every six months, Rottweilers, and also other breeds, will frequently come into season every four or five months, or in other cases at intervals of up to eight or nine months. It is impossible to lay down hard and fast rules.

At about the time you would expect her to come in season it will pay you to wipe her with a piece of cottonwool at intervals of forty-eight hours. The colour will show clearly if she is in season. Failure to spot the commencement of the season can mean that you are unable to book your chosen stud dog in time, or that you have a long and wasted journey. It can also cause considerable pandemonium with the local canine street boys if you take her for a walk in the High Street without realizing that she is in season. Obviously during her season you will ensure that she does not get herself mated to a casual male caller. Nature is inclined to ignore the mating for which you paid several hundred pounds, preferring her to take to next door's Labrador. In theory the colour should change from red to straw-coloured when she is ready to conceive. This does not always apply and you can find yourself waiting until she has finished her season without the colour clearing.

Let us assume that the colour does clear at about the eleventh to thirteenth day. Your bitch is standing close to the fence, on the other side of which your neighbour's Labrador is going demented. She is twitching her tail to one side and trying to push her rear end through the fence. Her very obvious reactions to the attentions of a male dog are the best indications that you can get that she is ready. You have already told the stud dog owners the approximate date you will require the mating. Now get on the telephone and tell them that you are coming tomorrow morning. Try and make it a calm and steady journey. It is no way to start by having the bitch vomiting all the way there and arriving a drooling wreck. Once there the stud dog owner will organize everything but will almost certainly require your assistance. We give details of the actual mating in Chapter 10, 'Stud Dogs and Stud Work'. Your job as her owner is to hold and calm her.

At the commencement of the tie your bitch may cry and whine for a few moments. This is quite normal and nothing to worry about. She will then settle down and stand quietly. Although it may not last very long both dogs and bitches frequently show considerable affection for each other during the mating and some males can be quite charming suitors.

The gestation period is sixty-three days during which you must wait patiently. There is nothing to be gained by rushing to the vet every few weeks to check whether she is in whelp. If she is not then there is nothing you can do about it until her next season. Above all do not allow your vet to X-ray her to see if she is carrying puppies. Putting X-rays through unborn puppies is the height of stupidity. Provided everything is proceeding normally there is no reason to go near your vet. The less your bitch is upset, by strange places and being pushed and poked around, the better.

During the first three weeks of pregnancy very little change of diet is necessary except for the addition of vitamin E which can either be a tablespoonful of Bemax or two wheat germ capsules. Canovel tablets are a good source of vitamins and minerals and most dogs like them. From the fourth week an addition of raspberry leaf tablets and garlic tablets help. The raspberry leaf tablets are a great assistance in a clean whelping and garlic tablets keep worms at bay, which can be transmitted by the bitch to the whelps when feeding. While some sceptics may raise their eyebrows at the use of raspberry and garlic they will certainly do no harm.

By the end of the fourth week the protein in the diet can be increased and an easy way of doing this is to add an egg to the food. The bitch will now be eating about two pounds of meat plus biscuit. No rigid amounts of food can be advised since much depends on the individual bitch, but common sense will tell you if she is getting sufficient. Beware of overfeeding since a fat bitch may experience difficulties in whelping. The aim is a well-fleshed bitch without excessive fat. By the end of the fifth or sixth week when you can see that she is in whelp, add more calcium. This can be given in the form of bonemeal. Two good meals a day morning and evening are generally sufficient, but if she is very heavy and looks to be having a large litter, these may be split into three smaller meals a day. With Rottweilers we find they exercise normally up to the birth date, and this is all to the good since healthy muscle tone contributes to an easy whelping. Again common sense must prevail and no exceptionally strenuous jumping or twisting be allowed.

About ten days before she is due to whelp move the bitch into the whelping room. She needs to have accepted this as her nursery well beforehand. Also, during the week or so before she whelps, make sure that she is not making her own whelping nest somewhere else. Bitches will sometimes dig themselves a hole under a building or in some other hidden spot. You do not want to have to pull the house down because she and her puppies are tucked away in the foundations.

The whelping box will need an overhead heater of the dull emitter type. Do not use the infra-red type which involves a glass lamp-bulb giving out a red glow. These can break and broken glass all over your puppies is not a good idea. The type we find best is a lump of fireclay in the shape of an electric light bulb. The element is imbedded in it and it screws into a reflector base. The whole thing is hung by a chain over the box, and can be raised or lowered as required.

For bedding at this stage we suggest clean flat newspaper in a thick layer all over the box. You will need mountains of newspaper so save it all and ask your friends to do the same. On top of the newspaper use one of the proprietary dog beds which can be bought in the size you require. Vet Bed or Dri Bed are two well-known makes. You will require at least three pieces, one in use, one in the wash, and one ready for use. These products have the ability to allow moisture to pass through to the newspaper underneath while the top surface remains dry and warm. Use pieces which cover only about half the box area. You may find that the bitch feels too warm on the bedding and prefers to lie on the uncovered area while leaving the puppies on the warm bed.

Some breeders use rails in the whelping box, so arranged

that the bitch cannot squash a puppy against the side wall. Use them if you wish but we do not believe that a bitch will squash a puppy in this way and that so-called 'lain on' puppies have in fact died from some other reason and their presence is then ignored by the bitch. When a live and fit puppy is behind or beneath a bitch you will find she is aware of it and is putting no weight on it.

She will start to make her nest during the days immediately prior to whelping and all your carefully spread out newspaper will probably be torn up and scratched into a heap. This is probably the first sign that she is close to whelping.

Rottweiler bitches are normally very punctual and whelp on the sixty-third day or close to it. However, it is not unusual for them to whelp four or five days early or to delay for a similar period.

Before the whelping day is due, make sure you have all the things ready that may be necessary. Below is a list of things which you will need.

On a tray:
1. One pair of blunt-ended scissors (sterilized)
2. White thread (sterilized)
3. Lots of squares of clean towelling
4. Bowl of water. Dettol and cloth
5. Plastic bucket
6. Newspapers
7. Hot water bottles
8. Small cardboard carton or basket

We have found, almost without exception, that Rottweilers are easy whelpers. This is probably due to two reasons. One is the fact that they are a muscular, active breed, and the other is that the whelps are comparatively small at birth. However, it is as well to notify your vet in advance of the date of whelping in case you have to call him out in the middle of the night. In some breeds bitches will refuse food for twenty-four hours prior to whelping, but as most Rottweiler owners will tell you, this is not necessarily true of Rottweilers. We have had bitches which would wolf down a large meal ten minutes before producing their first puppy. A more definite sign is a general restlessness, getting in and out of the whelping box and scratching at the floor and obviously not being able to settle comfortably.

Some bitches are determined to have their first puppy in the place of their choice, usually your bed or the best sofa. Refusal to allow her to do this may mean that she will retain the puppy too long for its survival. If you do have this problem we can only suggest that you do all that you can to protect bed or sofa and allow her to have the first one where she wishes. Once this one is born you will find that you can move both puppy and bitch into the whelping box where she will settle down and produce the rest. This problem sometimes occurs because she has not been moved and settled in the whelping room well in advance.

Owners sometimes complain that the bitch is wandering around the house looking for a place to whelp. When you ask why she is not in her whelping room the reply is that she keeps coming out. We are afraid that the answer they get is, 'Well, shut the door.' All the same, do not let her feel that she is shut away as a punishment. During the period prior to whelping take her out for her usual exercise and spend time in the room with her, telling her what a nice place it is.

There are exceptional cases. One bitch we whelped refused point blank to whelp anywhere but in the garden, complete with vocal accompaniments. Before each puppy arrived she would go to the door to be let out and rush up to Charles' kennel with loud barks, repeating the performance at Rachel's kennel. This violent activity would bring on the contractions, whereupon she would squat in the middle of the lawn, one of us would catch the puppy in a towel and we would all return to the whelping room to await the next performance. Ten puppies were born in this way.

Returning to our normal whelping and assuming that she is content to have them where you want, in the box, she will commence panting, and when this becomes very heavy, this is the time when you should be close at hand as the birth is imminent.

Particularly with a bitch having her first litter, the presence of her owner can be very reassuring and calming, and can encourage the bitch to get on with the job in hand. This heavy panting will lead on to contractions quite quickly. These will become stronger, and just before the puppy is born the water bag will burst, and shortly after this the puppy will arrive. Usually he will come enclosed in a transparent membrane which must be broken open immediately to free the head and enable the puppy to take his first breath. The puppy will still be attached to the cord, and at the end of this is the placenta. At this stage the bitch is more interested in chewing through the cord and eating the placenta than in 'unpacking' her puppy, which is why we prefer to free the puppy ourselves. After swallowing the placenta, she will then be interested in licking and stimulating her puppy, which will probably crawl to a teat and begin sucking. If the bitch is unable or unwilling to bite the cord herself, then tie the cord with a piece of thread and cut with the sterile scissors between thread and placenta. A fairly frequent occurrence is the breech presentation when the puppy comes hind feet first. A puppy in this position often takes longer to be delivered, and it is possible to assist the bitch by taking hold of the puppy's feet when these can be seen protruding, with a clean piece of towel, and pulling gently in a downward direction during a contraction. Often the bag has already broken before the puppy is born and he may have already inhaled some of the fluid, so delivery must be effected as soon as possible so that the lungs can be cleared. This can be done by holding the puppy firmly, supporting his head and swinging him rapidly through an arc downward from above your head to the floor. This will force fluid out of the lungs down the puppy's nose and will cause him to gasp. Wipe the liquid from the nose and repeat the procedure several times. Continue to stimulate the puppy with a rough towel until he is moving and breathing.

Quite frequently, especially with a maiden bitch, her first puppy will come as a surprise and shock for her. She may believe that she has done something wrong and even be frightened by him. You may find her sitting as far away as possible staring at the object which has suddenly appeared. If this happens first attend to the puppy, at the same time praising her and telling her how clever she is. Show her the puppy and let her lick it while still praising her. Do not, under any circumstances, scold her for what you may consider to be a failure in her maternal duties. Rottweiler bitches, unlike some breeds who will not whelp while you are present, appear to welcome and take comfort from their owner's presence during whelping.

When all is proceeding normally leave the first puppy

with the bitch until a number have been born. As more arrive remove some of the first ones to a warm box; this is when you use well-covered hot water bottles in a carton or basket. If you leave all the puppies with her, the early ones wil be soaked by the new arrivals' water bags each time and this is an unnecessary discomfort for them. Sometimes contractions slow down and a cold drink of milk with glucose in it may be given, followed by a brisk trot round outside; this will usually start things moving again. Although Rottweilers are very easy whelpers, should the bitch strain for a couple of hours without results, or the contractions cease altogether, do not hesitate to call your veterinary surgeon. A good maxim is: 'When in doubt, call him out.' If the litter is a large one, try to prevent the bitch from eating all the afterbirths as this may give her diarrhoea; four or five are sufficient and are probably good for her. Remove the others and wrap in newspapers to be disposed of. Be very careful to count all the afterbirths as obviously there should be one for each puppy, and a retained afterbirth can give a great deal of trouble and cause an infected uterus which would need immediate veterinary attention. Do not panic if you find that not all the afterbirths have cleared straight away. Some may not clear for twenty-four hours or so. However, if any are missing keep an eye open for any signs of trouble.

When the last puppy has arrived your bitch will relax, and now is the time to put all her warm dry babies with her. See that they all get to a teat and are sucking strongly. If necessary hold them to a teat, squeeze a little milk from the teat, gently opening the puppy's mouth and putting it over the teat and hold it there until it is sucking strongly. You can give the bitch a drink of warm milk and honey and leave her to rest and recuperate. She will probably sleep very soundly for a couple of hours. A Rottweiler can manage eight or nine puppies adequately, but more than this may need supplementary feeding with a bottle two or three times a day, although nothing is as good for the puppies as the bitch's own milk.

For the first few days the bitch will be most reluctant to leave the puppies and you must be firm and make her go outside to relieve herself. A light diet for the first day consisting of milk and eggs, etc., and lots of water to drink, especially with a large litter. With Rottweilers the bitch is rapidly back on a protein diet: Rottweiler puppies take enormous quantities of milk from the mother and one can hardly feed her too much. A good rule is to feed to appetite. Equally important is an adequate supply of calcium. Continue with the additives used during pregnancy and increase the bonemeal and calcium from the second week onwards.

On the third day we remove the dewclaws, which are sometimes found on the hind legs as well as the front. You may prefer to ask your veterinary surgeon to do this, but it is quite a simple operation to do yourself. You will need a helper and a tray with sterilized scissors, a saucer of crushed permanganate of potash crystals (obtainable from a chemist) and some damp cotton wool swabs. Get your helper to hold his thumb firmly above the dewclaw to stop the circulation, then cut through the base of the dewclaw and quickly apply the potash with the cotton wool swab. Release the pressure after a few seconds and there should be no loss of blood. The following day we dock the tails, preferring the rubber band method. Take the rubber bands, approximately an eighth of an inch wide, and cut them through so that you have the required number of rubber strips. Have your helper hold the puppy with the tail extended towards you, put the band under the tail just below the level of the anus, bring the ends of the band round the tail and tie as tightly as you can. If you have done this correctly the circulation will be cut off and the tail will shrivel and drop off in three to four days. The reason we prefer this method is that there is so little distress and no loss of blood to the puppy that it can be done with the mother in the room. If the tail drops off whilst the bitch is attending the puppy, she will often swallow it with no ill effects. The other method of docking is cutting, and this of course should be done by a veterinary surgeon. This is more painful to the puppy although quick, and should never be done within earshot of the mother. The nails of the puppies grow very fast and should be clipped once a week with nail scissors, otherwise the bitch may get some very painful scratches on the teats as the puppies feed. When the litter is about three weeks old, weaning should commence; start at two weeks if the litter is very large. Begin with raw scraped beef. Take a lean piece of beef and a teaspoon, and scrape the teaspoon down the grain of the meat leaving all the stringy bits behind. The resulting scraped meat is very soft and delicate and easily digestible. About half a teaspoonful of this per puppy is enough to begin with; put it on the finger and allow the puppy to sniff it. Most Rottweilers will eat it avidly, especially if they are not perhaps getting a lot of milk. If they are at all hesitant gently put it in their mouths. Increase the quantity daily, the next day a teaspoonful, building up gradually to two ounces at five weeks. By five weeks the meat need no longer be scraped but can be finely minced. If the mother has not got a lot of milk, commence with a milk feed for the puppies as early as two weeks. Give about a tablespoon mixed with baby cereal and a spot of honey. Do not use cow's milk – it is not nearly rich enough – but use evaporated milk or dried milk made for puppies, and make the consistency that of pouring cream, not too liquid. Gradually work the feeds up until four are being given daily, alternate milk and meat. After the first week of supplementary feeding, begin adding vitamin drops and bonemeal to the meat meal. One of the milk feeds can be a milk pudding with an egg added, the white of which should be cooked. You should allow one egg for every three puppies to begin with. Add a good quality puppy meal to the meat from about five weeks. Quantities should be increased as the puppies grow. Continue with four meals daily until they are at least four months old.

Rottweiler puppies do not always thrive on a diet containing too much milk or milk substitutes. If you find that your puppies' motions are loose then try cutting out one or even both of the milk feeds and substitute solids.

You may prefer to use one of the various proprietary puppy foods on the market. Many of them are quite satisfactory and can be used in accordance with the makers' instructions. If you do use such a product the Pedigree Petfoods Puppy Meat plus Mixer is probably the best. Avoid the cheaper products. We have found that the so called 'all-in-one' diets, even if expensive, are not ideal for Rottweiler puppies, tending to produce overweight puppies and sometimes digestive troubles. If you do use an all-in-one product alternate the meals with a certain amount of fresh meat, eggs and milk dishes.

Do not use any feeding system which leaves food available

to the puppies at all times, labour saving as it may appear. Meals should be prepared in the right quantities and eaten under your supervision. If you are getting it right there should be none left over after a couple of minutes. If there is any left over take it away and adjust your quantities for next time. Make sure that there is plenty of room round the dish so that the big puppies do not push the small ones out. The circular feeding dishes shaped like a shallow bell are very useful.

An important point to remember is to worm the puppies, usually between the third and fourth week. The best product we have found is Shaw's Earli-worm. This is a pleasant tasting liquid and one teaspoonful is sufficient; they swallow it without any bother. This dose should be repeated in ten days' time. The bitch should now be spending longer periods away from the puppies during the day and by the time they are five weeks old should only be with them at night. By six weeks the pups will be completely weaned and most Rottweiler bitches are only too happy to relinquish their babies at this age.

As the puppies are taking less from the mother, her food should be cut down, especially the milk-producing liquids and the extra meat.

It is worth noting the growth rate of a Rottweiler puppy. This never ceases to amaze us: from the time he is conceived he increases in weight to approximately sixteen ounces by the time he is born sixty-three days later, but during the next sixty-three days he can gain over fifteen pounds. So you can see how important it is to feed the bitch and puppies unstintingly. A puppy that is inadequately fed during the first few months will rarely make up into a good show or breeding proposition, and it is essential that a working dog should have a strong healthy body.

Almost as important as food for the puppies is fresh air. After three weeks let them have freedom to totter about, and if the weather is good, sunshine is especially beneficial; short airings outside in the warmth will do them immense good. Take full advantage of any sunny spells, but avoid two dangers – damp and draughts. Try to find a sheltered spot, perhaps on a blanket against a warm wall. If the sun is very strong, make sure they have shade – hot sun is very uncomfortable for young puppies. As well as fresh air, socializing is of great importance. If the puppies have not actually been born in the house, as soon as possible get their pen close to the house where they can become used to the comings and goings. Talk to them, allow the house dogs to snuffle at them through the wire, in short get them used to as many things as possible. We believe that puppies should have plenty of living space. They cannot develop to their full potential either physically or mentally under cramped conditions.

Nature attempts to bridge the gap between mother's milk and eating solid food by giving the bitch the instinct to regurgitate her own partly digested food for her puppies to eat. Apart from making your nice clean puppies and box into a revolting mess this deprives the bitch of nourishment which she needs and is of no benefit to the puppies as you are providing a suitable diet. If at the weaning stage your bitch does this, and many do, then feed her away from the puppies and keep her away for an hour or so.

Some bitches will take all the extra food that you give them and 'put it on their own backs', growing fatter and sleeker each day while passing little nourishment on to their puppies. Others will produce a copious milk flow and fade away to skin and bone. No breeder to our knowledge has ever attempted to produce a strain of bitches with their milking capacity as a priority. There are too many problems involved. However, it may pay you to reconsider breeding a second or third time from a bitch who does not do her puppies well. Neither should you be ashamed of a bitch who loses condition as a result of her efforts to do the best for her young, provided that you in your turn have done everything you can to keep her well fed and nourished.

It is quite normal for a bitch to go into a heavy moult after a litter. Regular grooming helps to clear away the dead hair and she will soon revert to her normal glossy self.

No puppy should be removed from the litter, to be sold or for any other reason other than illness, until it is at least seven weeks old.

We do not subscribe to the division of mental development into precise periods, even measured by exact numbers of days. Puppies, like any other living creature, develop at varying rates. Some are more precocious than others. We do however, accept that up to about seven weeks the puppy needs the security of dam and litter mates. After this time he is ready gradually to discover the world outside. Obviously the vital word is gradually. In natural conditions the puppy would first put a cautious nose outside the nest, then growing a little bolder would creep outside, ready to dart back at the first sign of danger. The next stage would be playing in the immediate vicinity, slowly increasing the area of familiarity until he was ready to face the big wide world.

Mentally, after seven weeks, the future adult dog starts to be formed. This is the time when he will begin to learn about his relationship with other dogs and humans. We, therefore, like our puppies to go to their new homes at between seven and nine weeks of age, thus learning the ways of their new owners. The breeder must give any puppy that does not go by this age the attention he would have received from his new owner. One sometimes sees the remainder of litters which have not been sold: perhaps five or six wild young teenagers, given no opportunity to develop their full mental capacity and rapidly reaching the stage where they will be uncontrollable.

The problems of finding suitable owners for your puppies and their future upbringing are covered in Chapter 5, 'Living with a Rottweiler'. At this stage we hope that you have achieved a healthy, well-reared litter already accustomed to being handled, responsive, and not frightened by the human voice or by domestic sights and sounds.

10

Stud Dogs and Stud Work

Several times a year someone will contact us and offer, as a
great favour, the opportunity to use his dog on one of our
bitches. The reasons given vary from: 'I thought it would be
kind to let him do it once', or 'He is always trying to mate the
cat or the children', or 'He is such a nice dog it seems a pity
that he does not father some puppies.' It is often difficult to
remain polite while explaining that our bitches are not there
to assuage the lust of his dog. That his dog is a poor
specimen, and if he values the welfare of the breed he will
never allow him to be used on any bitch. That the pedigree
does not fit our breeding plans and furthermore that what
the dog has never had he will not miss, or at least not miss so
much. Also that dogs used at stud tend to become more
dominant and aggressive, and that stud work means that the
dog will 'mark' all over the house, and that the owner will
start to complain that the dog has become dirty indoors.

The whole basis of pedigree dog breeding is that man con-
trols it. Take away this control and you will very quickly
cease to have all the various breeds that we know. You will
merely have dogs. You will have lost any opportunity of
being able to predict the temperament and physical characteristics of a given breed or, within a breed, of any particular
bloodline. Everyone buying a dog will be in the same position as the purchaser of a dear little cuddly fluffy mongrel
puppy who is later horrified to find that he grows into an
enormous, hairy brute who destroys the furniture and bites
the postman. Neither is it sufficient to say that both parents
are Rottweilers and that it is acceptable to mate any
Rottweiler dog to any Rottweiler bitch. Serious breeders
will spend a lifetime trying to improve their breed. Trying to
ensure that the stock they produce will conform with their
idea of what is desirable both in conformation and temperament. The high quality that such breeders produce can very

quickly be lost if bitches are mated to the 'dog next door'. The use of an inferior male merely because he is easily available, or offered at a cheap stud fee, can never be condoned. Those who breed in such a way, without regard to the quality of the puppies they produce, are guilty of reducing dog breeding to a despicable commercial operation, the sole justification for which is greed. None of what we have just said should be interpreted as a demand that only the famous and successful stud dogs from well-known kennels should be used. For those new to the breed such dogs certainly offer the safest and best chance of success. However, if you genuinely believe that a dog, unknown as he may be, can help you breed your ideal Rottweiler then by all means use him, but remember that while you may take the acclaim for success you must also bear the responsibility for failure.

We hope that the foregoing will convince you that choosing a stud dog for your bitch, or deciding to allow your male to be used, is not a matter to be undertaken lightly. We discussed the desirable temperament of bitch owners in Chapter 9, 'Breeding – Whelping and Rearing'. If you are considering becoming a Rottweiler stud dog owner you should be aware that it is not just a question of owning a suitable dog and counting the stud fees.

The mating of two animals the size of Rottweilers can be painful, to the back, knees, muscles and temper. We are talking about the effect on the humans involved, not the dogs. We have seen strong men wince and turn pale at the sight of the dog tying and turning. Furthermore, as we will explain later, it will probably require the assistance of three people. Not for Rottweiler breeders the mating on the kitchen table, with dog in one hand and cup of tea in the other, as enjoyed by toy dog breeders. With Rotts it can be hard, dirty, exhausting work.

If, in spite of what we have said, you decide that your male is good enough to be used and, more importantly, that there is a demand for his services, then you must decide on the terms and conditions which you will apply. The simple rule of thumb for calculating a stud fee used to be that the fee would be roughly the same as the average price of a puppy. However, because you paid a very high price for a top quality dog puppy it does not automatically follow that his

stud fee will be the same. Stud fees, like puppy prices, are to
a great extent covered by the law of supply and demand. In
other words the price is what you can get. In general, stud
fees are, at the time of writing, running at about two-thirds
of puppy prices. Outstanding stud dogs may very well be
able to demand a fee higher than this. Stud dogs offered at
very low prices are almost certainly not worth using
although regrettably they may be used far more, because of
their low fee, than more worthy animals.

It is possible for a stud dog owner to make any terms or
conditions he may wish. Whether bitch owners will accept
them is another matter. If you are wise, you will remain
within the conventions which are usually acceptable to dog
breeders. These are, that the stud dog owner has the right to
refuse to allow his dog to be used on a bitch he does not
approve of; that the fee is payable at the time of mating,
assuming that the mating took place in a satisfactory manner, which in our opinion should include an adequate tie;
that a free second mating will be given at a subsequent
season if puppies do not result from the mating.

There are a number of points which arise from these conventions. Some stud dog owners, jealous of their dogs'
reputations, will only allow their use on bitches which they
consider to be of high quality. This of course enhances a
dog's reputation for producing good stock. Others, and we
incline to this view, will argue that it is the function of an
outstanding sire to improve the overall standard of the
breed, and that it is better that he should be used to upgrade
breed quality by his use on bitches of only average merit,
rather than see the general breed standard reduced by the
same bitch going to a mediocre male.

With dogs, unlike horses where the convention is 'no foal
no fee', this is, as we have said, payable at the time of a successful mating. The only common exception to the rule is in
the case of an unproven stud dog. Serious breeders will
usually not put a dog at stud until he has sired a litter to one
of their own bitches. They not only wish to know that he is
capable of producing puppies but that the puppies are of
satisfactory quality. A further and understandable reason is
that if the male starts to sire outstanding puppies they wish
to be the first to unveil them in the show ring. Failure to

conceive is probably connected with the bitch rather than the dog. Some bitch owners will ask for a second mating at no extra charge some forty-eight hours after the first. While you may be quite willing to agree to this, in our experience it makes no difference to the size of the subsequent litter. Bitches that have been allowed to run with males while in season and have been mated a number of times will still only produce a normal sized litter. What you do is to increase your chances of mating the bitch on the day at which she is at the highest level of ovulation. If you feel that the bitch is absolutely ready at the first mating then there is little point in having a second. If, however, the bitch allowed the mating, but only under a certain amount of protest, then a second mating may be desirable. Still on the subject of the bitch owners getting what they have paid for, we consider that the mating should take place with the bitch owner present. Firstly, because if the bitch owner is too squeamish to be present then it is doubtful whether he or she is a suitable person to breed Rottweilers anyhow, and secondly, because it will be helpful if her owner is there to hold and calm the bitch during what can be a traumatic occurrence. There is a third reason. Not all stud dog owners are as scrupulous as one would wish and it is not unknown for a stud dog owner to suggest that the bitch owner should stay by the fire while the bitch is taken away to be mated. Half an hour later when the bitch is brought back the owner has no proof that she has in fact been mated to the desired dog or even that she has been mated at all. Travel problems, timing, etc. may on occasions justify a bitch being left in the stud kennel for mating. As a general rule we suggest that you try and avoid it.

Again on the subject of money we do not like the 'puppy in lieu of stud fee' arrangement. If the bitch owner cannot afford the stud fee then they probably cannot afford to rear the puppies properly. Neither do we like the 'reduced stud fee plus one or more puppies' deal, as it often results in the bitch owners paying an exorbitant fee. Such arrangements almost invariably lead to trouble: the stud dog owners wanting the only dog or bitch in the litter – the very one that the bitch owners have set their hearts on. Stud payments, like puppy sales, should be on a straightforward 'goods in exchange for cash' basis.

Finally on the question of allowing a repeat mating at a subsequent season if the bitch has missed to the original mating: there is no obligation to do this. However, most reputable breeders will do so, and whether or not this is agreeable should be clearly stated before the first mating takes place.

The next question you must ask yourself is where the mating should take place. The convention is that the bitch goes to the dog. There are a number of reasons for this. Stud dog owners will, or should have, suitable facilities. Secondly, owners of well-known stud dogs are probably busy people with a lot of dog interests. They will not take kindly to travelling long distances for the dog to be used. After all, they are probably the ones who have spent years developing their bloodlines. If you want their bloodlines you will have to go to them. 'Have stud dog, will travel' is an advertising approach sometimes seen. The true interpretation of this is that the owners are either desperate for the money or it is the only way that they can persuade people to use the dog. Equally, and bitch owners should bear this in mind, do not pester every bitch owner, saying that he should use your dog on his bitch. It is the same approach as the saleswoman who says, 'Madam looks absolutely beautiful in this £5000 fur coat.' The aim is to sell the coat or the dog, whichever applies. If they ask, you should advise bitch owners of the probable results of a particular mating. If you are honest you may even recommend someone else's dog, if you do not think that your own is suitable for that particular bitch. The golden rule is to allow the bitch owner to decide what dog they wish to use, and in the long run your reputation will be far higher if you offer genuine unprejudiced advice rather than constantly pushing the merits of your dog.

After this long homily on the problems of owning a stud dog, you are probably wishing that we would get back to Rottweilers. Let us assume that you have a dog puppy, that he is an excellent specimen with a good pedigree and that if you support the principle of line-breeding he has been so bred in the hope that the characteristics which make him good are inherent in him.

Obviously you will rear him carefully so that he develops into a strong, fit dog. Apart from his physical well-being you must also take care that his psychological welfare is given attention. He is going to meet strange bitches and even more important, strange humans. He must be accustomed to being handled, helped, lifted and restrained. A dog who is not willing to accept close contact with humans during mating can become protective of a bitch, refuse to be helped and even attack anyone whom he considers is interfering with his mating of the bitch. Such a dog will rapidly become unusable as a stud dog. From puppyhood onwards you will probably find that he indulges in sex play, trying to mate other puppies or clasping your leg in an amorous embrace. Embarrassing as this may be it is essential that you do not discourage him. If, for the first eighteen months of his life, he is scolded for obeying his natural instincts then it is not surprising if he is unwilling to do what is expected of him when you wish him to. He will probably be a trifle precocious during adolescence; again you must protect him from being told off if he gets a little too ambitious and makes advances to an adult dog without due cause. If you are an obedience or working trial enthusiast you may give yourself problems. We have seen a highly trained Rottweiler who refused to mate a very willing bitch as long as his owner was present. He had been taught that he must not do such things. When we realized what the problem was and sent the owner away the dog performed immediately.

So you now have a young, fit, male Rott. At what age should he first be used? A male as young as nine months will successfully mate a bitch. A thought to remember if you have your young dog kenneled with a bitch. In our opinion no Rottweiler should be used before about twelve months of age and then only occasionally. A Rott is by no means mature until about two years old and has quite a lot of growing to do between twelve and twenty-four months. Many breeders do, however, use a dog for the first time at about one year. This is not only because we get impatient to see what he can produce, but also because it helps to get him started while he is still relatively gentle and easy-going. It is helpful if his first bitch is older and has been mated before. Two young, frisky Rottweilers, neither quite sure what it is all about, will give you lots of problems, particularly if you are also inexperienced.

You will need a suitable area for your matings. Keeping

them both on leads rapidly results in everyone being tied up in a tangle. Let them loose in a large field and both the dogs and yourselves will be exhausted before the mating starts. The ideal is a fenced compound about twenty-five feet square. It is useful to have electric light. Many bitch owners arrive after finishing work and when it is pitch dark. It is also a useful luxury if there is a roof over it. Clasping two Rottweilers in the pouring rain for half an hour can put you off canine sex for a long time. The most suitable venue is out of sight of neighbours or casual visitors. To have the vital moments viewed by either the vicar, a family complete with children, or a row of leering building workers can be discouraging to the dog and embarrassing to yourself.

Many owners ask too much of their dogs when they want to mate them. They expect them to mate the moment they are introduced so that their owners can get back indoors for a cup of tea. Both dog and bitch will normally indulge in a certain amount of foreplay before actually mating. With two Rottweilers this foreplay is something akin to two baby elephants learning to dance. With eyes only for each other they will hurl themselves around the compound scattering humans in all directions. For this reason you cannot keep either dog on a lead. It will very quickly be wound around your legs. Also, before you even introduce them to each other, put a strong flat leather collar on the bitch. Not a choke chain or a slip. The reason for this we will explain later. The foreplay may go on for some minutes. The dog is trying to talk her into it and she is deciding whether she approves of him or not. If, after some minutes of foreplay, the bitch turns and snaps at the dog, there are two likely reasons. Firstly, she may not be ready. She will know better than you whether she is ovulating and therefore able to conceive. The universal rule used to be that the mating should take place on the twelfth day after the first coloured discharge. This is not necessarily true and can only be a rough guide. In our own experience the time when a bitch will allow herself to be mated and will conceive can vary from the eighth day of the season to the twenty-third. When a bitch is ready she will usually make it very obvious. She will stand with back legs braced and quite deliberately twitch her tail to one side. The second reason she may reject the male's advances is simply because she is nervous and possibly spoilt. Bitches who live as the only pet in the household, unused to contact with other dogs, are often resentful of the dog's approaches. You now have to decide which of these two reasons is the relevant one. If it is just nervous bad temper then her natural instincts will probably give her away. Her tail will still twitch and she will stand but will snap as soon as the dog tries to mount her. If she is not ready then the tail will stay tucked down and she will try to escape from the dog. If you decide that she is not ready then the only thing to do is to send the owners away and ask them to bring her back in about forty-eight hours. Interrogate the owner as to when they first saw the coloured discharge. Some owners decide that the right day is the day that suits them, not the day that suits nature and the bitch.

Let us assume that it is the right day and that the bitch is just being awkward. Many Rottweiler bitches are very awkward. Your first action is to get the bitch owner to steady her by holding her by the collar while standing in front of her. He should use both hands, one either side of the head, and talk to her gently and try to calm her apprehension. If you are lucky the dog will mount and mate her. More likely, although she is held by the head, the bitch will sit down, making it impossible for the dog. At this stage you bring in your second assistant who, standing or more probably kneeling alongside the bitch, supports her under the tummy with one hand. It may be possible to put a knee under her, but the dog will often look at the collection of arms and legs and, if he could speak, say, 'Get out of the way, there is no room for me.' While the second assistant supports her with one hand it helps if his other hand is holding one of her hind legs, otherwise she may move her hindquarters sideways and everyone is going around in circles. So far the two humans involved need strength rather than skill. The third attendant, working on the free side of the bitch, needs to be both patient and skilful. Using one hand to press upwards on the bitch's tummy, just in front of the vulva, it is possible to move the vulva upwards while at the same time guiding the dog in. This must be done by guiding rather than forcing. Any attempt to force the dog forward will make him draw back. At last he is there; hold him by supporting his hindquarters for about a minute. They are now 'tied', or at least one hopes they are. It is still too early to relax. Very soon the male will probaby show signs of wishing to turn. Remember that the bitch and probably your helpers are supporting virtually all the weight of the dog, and with a fully grown male Rott this is no small weight. The male will start to move to one side or the other of the bitch. Move one of his forelegs over the bitch's back so that both his forelegs are located on one side of her. Then gently bring his rear leg over her back and allow him to turn so that they are facing opposite ways. Because of the weight and size of the dogs and the number of humans involved, this stage must be done gently, firmly and quickly. Make sure that he has room to turn around and that everyone moves quickly out of his way. There can be an awful tangle of arms, legs and dogs if this stage is not efficiently organized. You can now try to relax: one person still holding the bitch by her collar, a second holding the dog by his and the third person, the unlucky one, clasping the hind legs of both Rotts holding them together. The dog cannot move away from the bitch. Her muscles are gripping him and he has to remain until she releases her grip. The tie can last for a considerable time. Twenty minutes is quite normal but it may be less or considerably longer. Eventually she will let go, and the dog will probably sit or lie down and lick himself; the bitch will probably want to investigate what has been going on. Put her straight away into a kennel or back in her owner's car. Do not allow her to gallop around revelling in her sudden freedom from restraint. There is no need to pick her up by the hind legs, lay her down, or any other method of ensuring retention of the sperm which folklore claims are necessary. Just put her somewhere quiet where she can relax. Allow your dog to clean himself and fully retract before taking him back to his kennel.

Having had your successful mating there is one item of paper work that you should do. Assuming that the bitch owner intends to register the puppies with the Kennel Club, it is necessary that the stud dog owner signs the relevant K.C. form to the effect that the mating has taken place, giving details of the K.C. registration of the sire and the date of mating. This can also constitute your receipt for the stud fee. Registration cannot take place unless the certificate is completed. If payment is made by cheque it is reasonable that this form should be withheld until the cheque has been passed. People have been known to bounce cheques for stud fees. At the same time, or by the time the puppies are born, you should also give the bitch owner a copy of the stud dog's pedigree. In the wrong hands these documents can be misused and you should be sure not to leave out details such as the date of mating, and also check to ensure that the documents you have issued are applied to the correct litter.

Now for some of the problems you might have. It is essential that everyone should be calm, confident and patient. Remember that the bitch owner may be even more nervous than the bitch. Someone once described taking their Rottweiler bitch for mating. Immediately on arrival the stud dog owner seized the bitch, tied her collar tightly to a fence post, threw an old tin bath under her to support her, and said, 'Right, get on with it, I'm in a hurry.' Not the best way to go about it.

If the bitch persists in snapping at the dog, or even tries to bite you or her owner, and provided that you are satisfied that she is ready, then it may be necessary to muzzle her either with a proper muzzle or with a bandage. If you use a bandage loop it over her muzzle crossing it under her chin and then take it back behind her ears and tie it in a fairly tight bow knot. She can still breathe but cannot bite. Do not let a loving owner take the bandage off just as they are tied. An owner did this to us once and the bitch very nearly gave one of us a nasty bite in the face.

With the wide variations in height between Rottweiler males and bitches you may find difficulty in lining everything up. The dog may be too high for the bitch or too short and unable to reach. A convenient step may solve the problem or you may keep handy a wooden platform about 2 ins to 3 ins in thickness. This platform should be big enough for the bitch to stand on with all four feet and should be firm and rigid. Neither the dog nor the bitch will be happy if the ground moves under their feet. Cover the board with an old piece of carpet so that their feet can get a grip. Avoid any smooth slippery surface. Even without the board a piece of carpet can help provided you can persuade them to stand on it. Obviously you place the board under the dog or bitch depending on which is too short.

We have already said how important it is to have a well-trained team. We have even rehearsed our kennel maids with the aid of two low coffee tables, one mounted on the other, to show who does what and where all the legs go.

If, after a reasonable period of foreplay, your stud dog decides to fool about and will still not mount her, it may help if you hold him away from her on a lead for a few minutes or shut him in an adjoining run where he can see her. The frustration and fear of missing his chance will build up and encourage him to get on with it when he is released.

The use of drugs, and in particular the steroid group, can cause your dog to become infertile. If you are tempted to improve his growth rate, or cure lameness, by the use of such products you should be aware that you may cause long-term damage by so doing. Not only are you harming your dog but you are cheating yourself and those who wish to use the dog.

You will probably have picked up most of the terminology involved from reading this chapter. One term you will come across is a 'broken tie'. This is what happens when the dog penetrates but is not gripped by the bitch. There are a number of reasons for this. The bitch may have an obstruction, she may not be quite ready or she may object and struggle so much that the dog cannot penetrate completely and is forced out. If this does happen it is probable that you will be unable to use the dog again for at least several hours. It should be obvious to you that it is most uncomfortable for the dog to walk in this condition and he should be left quietly where he is to rest and recover. Do not allow the bitch to pester him at this time. Once when this happened to us, we said in a frustrated voice, 'She's broken it.' 'Oh,' said the woman owner, staring at the dog with shocked horror, 'I didn't realize it was so fragile. Will it mend again?'

Finally, you may ask why all this fuss to achieve something which nature can cope with without any assistance. If a bitch in season gets out she will mate without human aid and produce a litter. Why not just shut the two of them in a run and let them get on with it? The main objection to this is that after they are 'tied' the bitch may struggle and drag the dog, causing serious injury to him. Secondly, it will almost certainly take very much longer, and you will all have to stand around for hours to satisfy yourselves that the mating has taken place.

11

Illness

There are many excellent books on canine diseases and their treatment. For the serious breeder and conscientious owner these are well worthwhile studying so that you may both understand and assist your vet, who must be your main advisor in such matters. In this chapter we have not attempted to cover the enormous range of illnesses which can affect the dog. What we have attempted to do is to discuss those complaints which are of particular relevance to the Rottweiler and to put such illnesses into a proper perspective.

One word of warning. Reading books on the diseases of the dog can, like reading medical dictionaries, create a hypochondriac owner. One vet with a fashionable London practice once said that in many cases the best treatment was an aspirin for the owner and nothing for the dog. As we have said, the Rottweiler is a healthy animal and the vast majority live a reasonable life span with very few problems. Regrettably, like all the larger breeds, the Rottweiler does not live as long as we would wish. Ten years old is about the average although many go to eleven or twelve. The record, as far as we know, is a dog from one of our early litters. This dog was born in this country, went to Germany with his owners, returned via quarantine and lived to the age of sixteen.

Distemper, Hardpad, Leptospirosis and Hepatitis

These diseases have all, in their time, been serious. If your dog got any of these then it would be seriously ill and might die. The prevention is quite simple. Your vet will inoculate your Rottweiler against these diseases, using a combined vaccine, probably administered at about twelve weeks of age, followed by annual boosters. Because inoculation pro-

grammes have been in common use for a considerable time
it is unusual today to hear of a dog suffering from any of
these diseases. Keep your inoculations up to date and you
should have no problems.

Parvovirus

This is a very different matter. This disease did not, as far as
is known, exist before 1977 and yet by 1980 it was a world-
wide scourge, killing many dogs in a horrible and painful
manner. The symptoms are loss of appetite, listlessness,
sickness and foul-smelling bloody diarrhoea. If your
Rottweiler shows any of these signs then call your vet as
quickly as possible.

For some reason still unknown, Rottweilers and one or
two other breeds seemed to be more susceptible to the disease and had a higher fatality rate. Not only unvaccinated
Rotts succumbed but others which had been vaccinated
with the vaccines then available. Drug manufacturers and
also the veterinary profession would not at first accept that
Rottweilers were more at risk than other breeds, until the
high loss rate convinced them that what breeders were saying was correct. The disease caused the greatest loss
amongst young stock from about ten weeks to eighteen
months of age.

Part of the problem was the natural immunity which the
puppy acquired from its mother. Immunity is measured by
what is known as the titre level. Roughly half the titre level
of the bitch is passed to the puppy. The titre level acquired
from the bitch decreases in the puppy at the approximate
rate of half every ten days. In other words if the bitch has a
level of 500, the puppy starts off with a level of 250 and at
the end of ten days has a level of 125. The natural immunity
acquired from the bitch can neutralize the injected vaccine.
You therefore have the problem of declining immunity
coupled with resistance to the vaccine. In addition, some of
the early vaccines did not seem to work with Rottweilers.
The breakthrough came with the introduction of a product
called Nobi-vac Parvo C. The second aid was the use of
blood tests on the puppies to establish the titre level. In the
state of knowledge at the time of writing we have established

a routine which so far has worked. The puppy is given first inoculations at six weeks. At eight to nine weeks he is given a blood test immediately followed by a further inoculation. Should the result of the blood test show a satisfactory titre level then you can stop there. If it does not, then repeat the process of blood test followed by inoculation at about twelve to fourteen weeks. If all goes well, both blood tests, and certainly the second, should show a satisfactory titre level. It is said that a titre level of about 4000 gives a life-time immunity. If this is achieved, and it usually is, then it is difficult to understand the need for annual boosters. However, the manufacturers recommend that you should and we would not advise you otherwise. You will find that some Rotts seem determined to have a low titre level. You may need to consider vaccinating beyond the given pro-gramme to achieve the desired result. You may also find that it is virtually impossible to raise the level above a hundred or so. If you do, do not worry: the resistance seems to be there even if it does not show by the current means of measure-ment. One final word of advice. Some vets will try to reduce the programme, or delay its commencement, while others will wish to use a vaccine combining the parvo vaccine with those for distemper etc. We insist that all the parvo shots are separate, having a theory that the combined shots may inhibit each other. We are probably wrong but it has worked for us.

At the time of writing this is our experience with parvo vaccines. Science moves fast and research is going on all the time. There is obviously much more to be learnt. What we learnt out of the parvo epidemic was that medicines are sold by salesmen and that their current product is always perfect until a better one is produced. We also formed the opinion that discount structures and other incentives make some of the veterinary profession inclined to suggest an existing product rather than a new and possibly unfamiliar one.

Entropion

This is a condition whereby the eyelids turn inwards causing the eyelashes to rub on the cornea and eventually cause ulcers. It is extremely painful for the dog, as you can imagine. While it is not common in Rottweilers there are some strains which carry this fault. Its eradication has not been helped by breeders using the operation to cure it, which is obviously desirable for the dog's sake, but continuing to show and breed from the animal in spite of the fact that the condition is hereditary. In the early days of Rottweilers in Britain the call for an almond eye, given in the Standard, led some breeders to confuse this requirement with an eye buried in heavy wrinkle, the shape that tends to produce entropion. The operation is fairly simple and almost invariably successful. Unfortunately, if well done, it is virtually undetectable. The condition can be recognized by a constantly weeping, half-closed eye. It is possible in very mild cases to cure it by the use of ointment, particularly in young dogs, when the skull has not fully developed. It is also possible that the symptoms can be reproduced by conjunctivitis or even, as exhibitors occasionally tell judges in the show ring, by the dog sitting with its head out of the window of the car. Selective breeding can virtually eliminate entropion within very few generations although the odd case may reappear. There is no excuse for breeders perpetuating entropion in Rottweilers.

Skin Troubles

Although your vet, when giving injections, will tell you that Rottweilers have thick skins, they are in fact remarkaby sensitive to insect bites and other skin irritations. A single flea bite on a Rottweiler will cause the dog to nibble and scratch at the spot and within a few hours you have a patch of wet eczema. If left unattended it will rapidly spread in a mess of pus over a large area from which the hair will fall out. The first indication is often a small wet patch of hair. Examine this and you will find underneath the first sign of eczema. You may also find signs of flea infestation around the same area. Bathe the affected area with a solution of household disinfectant, such as Dettol or Savlon, making sure you remove all pus. Dry and apply an ointment such as Germolene which is both antiseptic and a local anaesthetic. We have found this method effective in almost all cases provided you act before the eczema has become too deep-seated. It goes without saying that you should use an anti-parasitic product at the same time.

Young Rottweiler puppies will sometimes show signs of scurf on their coats which continues to appear in spite of repeated brushing. This is usually a sign of infection by a mite with the unpronounceable name of cheyletiella. Although the puppy almost certainly gets this infestation from his mother, the condition does not usually show on adults. An insecticidal shampoo, repeated a couple of times, will usually effect a cure very quickly. These mites can cause an irritating rash in some humans. One of the writers suffers in this way, and having come out in masses of little red spots on a number of occasions consulted our doctor who suggested, and tried, all sorts of cures without avail. In all cases the spots disappeared within 24 hours. Eventually we realized that the attacks coincided with picking up and cuddling puppies, and on asking our vet what effect cheyletiella had on humans, he said, 'Little red spots that itch like hell.' Do not worry: the mites are easily disposed of on puppies and do not persist on humans.

Scurf can also be caused by stress. A dog suddenly put into an unusual environment such as the show ring or boarding kennels can, in a very short time, produce scurf all over its head and body. If this happens just as you are about to enter the ring you will find that a frantic last minute brushing will only aggravate the problem. Use your silk polishing cloth to wipe the scurf gently off the surface of the coat.

Hip Dysplasia

H.D., which is the usual abbreviation, has become an extremely controversial subject during recent years. We have commented on the working of the H.D. scheme in Chapter 3, 'The Rottweiler in Great Britain'. We consider it to be only one of the problems which can affect Rottweilers and that its effect on the breed does not warrant some of the extreme attitudes which have been taken. Bearing in mind that all breeds existed and survived for many generations before H.D. was ever acknowledged to exist, we consider that the incidence of H.D. in Rottweilers, relative to other big breeds, shows that the Rott does not have too much to worry about. H.D. is the term used to describe the changes which occur in the hip joint, which is a ball and socket joint. The socket which is technically called the acetabulum can become too shallow to hold the ball, the head of the femur. This failure can vary from slight looseness to complete dislocation. While complete dislocation can cause lameness and pain, a degree of looseness, even though it may result in a substantial hip score (see below), appears to have very little effect on the dog's ability to lead a normal life. We think it unfortunate that considerable distress is caused to owners of much loved Rottweilers because, although showing no signs of trouble, they are diagnosed as suffering from H.D.

The BVA/KC scheme to assess H.D. in dogs works by the evaluation of an X-ray of the hips by a panel of veterinary orthopaedic specialists. They consider nine different aspects of the hip joint, each leg being calculated separately. Each aspect of the hip is scored up to a maximum of six points. '0' represents normality, six points indicates a high degree of deformity. The worst possible total score is therefore 54 or a total of 108 for both hips. The best possible score is 0.0 indicating normality in both hips.

We have mentioned that the breed average score is about 14. Admittedly the figure is arrived at by calculating the average for the Rottweilers put through the scheme. Roughly 12 per cent of Rottweilers registered with the Kennel Club are scored. Although this percentage may appear to be low you must remember that it represents a high percentage of the top stud dogs and brood bitches. Rottweiler breeders have an excellent record for their support for the scoring scheme. Only three breeds score a greater percentage of registrations.

Hip dysplasia is not entirely hereditary. To be more accurate the degree of H.D. which a dog may suffer is not solely the result of heredity. Expert opinion varies but a rough guide is that 60 per cent of the condition in a given dog is hereditary and 40 per cent is environmental. By environmental we mean such factors as injury at birth, slippery floors during rearing, diet, etc. No one has yet

'Calm gaze indicates good humour' – Chesara Dark Warpaint U.D.Ex.,
W.D. Certificate of Merit

These contented puppies have been docked by the rubber-band method

We shall soon be big enough to get over this gate

Puppy run. The gate in two halves aids control

Puppy run attached to whelping box

A useful puppy pen

Training for working trials: the 3-foot
clear jump

Excellent example of Rottweiler bitch
head *(Diane Pearce)*

The author awarding the Challenge Certificate to Ch. Rudi Anton Bali at
Crufts 1982

established clearly what environmental factors affect the final result. It was even suggested at one time that puppies kept in a totally restricted environment would not develop H.D. We doubt the truth of this and in any case we hate to think what other problems, both physical and of temperament, would result from this method. The statement that approximately 50 per cent of H.D. results from environment does not eliminate the hereditary factor or vice versa. The puppy will still inherit H.D. from his parents. It does mean that the final severity of H.D. in a given animal will be related to things that happen to him after he is born. A score which is 'lopsided', i.e. 0.20, meaning that one hip is normal while the other shows considerable deformity, is generally considered to be the result of injury at some stage of the dog's early life.

A complication which has now arisen is the requirement that the dog be given a general anaesthetic in order that it can be X-rayed. To position the dog for the X-ray requires that he is on his back with his legs drawn forwards and backwards. Not a position that many Rottweilers will accept when fully conscious. There have been a small number of cases where dogs have died under the anaesthetic. Because of this risk many breeders have used vets willing to X-ray using a sedative only and the assistance of the owner. All our own dogs have been X-rayed by this method. Changes in the safety regulations governing the use of X-rays have now made it very difficult to find a vet willing to X-ray without a general anaesthetic.

Breeders and breed clubs have, up to now, urged all owners to have their Rotts X-rayed for H.D. This has enabled a picture to be built up of the overall state of the breed and has produced valuable information as to the level of H.D. in the progeny of sires and dams. While we consider that it is still of great importance to score dogs used for breeding, especially sires who can have a great influence on the breed, we feel that it is morally wrong to urge the owner of a pet Rottweiler to put his dog at risk under a general anaesthetic for the sole purpose of furthering the scientific knowledge of the incidence of H.D. in the breed. The pet owner's Rottweiler is neither better nor worse as a result of being X-rayed. The risk of losing such a dog for reasons which give no benefit to either dog or owner is in our opinion unacceptable.

If you do decide to have your Rott X-rayed then please have it done under the official BVA/KC scheme which involves having the dog's Kennel Club registration number recorded on the plate at the time of taking the X-ray. Do not accept an assessment of the H.D. condition from the vet who takes the X-ray, unless of course he is one of the official scrutineers. Some vets are inclined to express an opinion which they are not qualified to give. It is not unusual for a vet to announce that the hips are good or 'not worth sending up'. In some cases their comments are the opposite to what is revealed when the plate is examined by the experts. We had one telephone call from a tearful owner saying that her vet had told her that her Rottweiler was suffering from severe H.D. When we asked her what the score was she told us that it was 2.2. She was a lot happier when we told her how lucky she was to have such a low score. If you do decide to put your Rott to the admittedly slight risk of X-raying then at least give the breed the benefit of the knowledge gained.

We would, therefore, urge you to treat H.D. as merely one of the many factors that you take into account when deciding to breed from a pair of Rottweilers. As a very well-known veterinary surgeon has said, 'Dogs did not have hip dysplasia until we learnt to recognize and treat it: they just had arthritis!' Many dogs, like humans, have arthritis in old age, including those with 0.0, scores.

Osteochondritis Dissicans

This condition, sensibly abbreviated to O.C.D., arises from faulty bone growth and causes lameness, most frequently in the shoulder, but to a lesser degree in elbow, stifle and hock. The faulty development of bone and cartilage can result in fragments dropping into the joint. The term tends to be used to cover a wide range of lameness, particularly in the forequarters, and one veterinary surgeon has said that much of such lameness can be described as growing pains. Certainly in many cases rest and restricted exercise can effect a permanent cure. The operation sometimes carried out to remove the fragments is not always successful, and while you should treat such lameness under veterinary supervision we would suggest rest and patience before agreeing to an operation.

Ruptured Cruciate Ligament

This is the rupture of the ligament which holds the stifle or knee joint together. It can occur during rapid movement possibly accompanied by the dog suddenly twisting or slipping. It has been suggested that apart from cases of immediate rupture, it is possible for the ligament to stretch gradually over a period of time and then suddenly fail. This may account for the number of occasions when the ligament ruptures when the dog is moving at a slow trot over a perfectly level surface. Rest and controlled exercise may cure the condition if the ligament is only strained, but in the case of complete rupture the surgical repair is extremely successful. While no evidence has been produced that the condition is hereditary, we prefer not to breed from stock that has suffered this injury, believing that some bloodlines show a tendency to do so.

We have devoted a considerable amount of space to orthopaedic problems in Rottweilers. We do not believe that they are any more prone to such illness than any other breed except in one respect: like footballers they are big heavy chaps who throw themselves around a lot and tend to suffer such injuries as a result. The answer, in our opinion, lies in breeding from sound stock, careful rearing on a good diet, and free exercise at the puppy's discretion, including rough-and-tumble games which allow muscle and bone to develop at the same time as weight.

Old Age

Rottweilers grow old gracefully. They slow down a little. Their roars of rage at their enemies become more of a habit

than a sign of aggression. The look of affection in their eyes
as they look at you reflects a certain wistfulness, as if they,
too, realize that your time together is slipping away. Grey
hairs around the muzzle come late in the Rott and apart
from a slight stiffness in the joints and a more sedate movement there is little to show that they are growing old. Often
deterioration is sudden, a matter of a week or so. You notice
that the flesh is falling away from the head, the skull bones
are more obvious, the hindquarters lose their round
muscular strength. Too often cancer is the cause of this
change. Many Rottweilers suffer its effects. We can offer
little help here except to say that most of them do not con-
tract the disease until late in life. At least one bitch we know
has so far had some two years of happy life after having one
leg, which had become cancerous, amputated. She has
learnt to live with only three legs and seems to suffer
little discomfort.

Care in old age is really common sense. Your pensioner
needs a warm dry bed, perhaps a little warmer and softer
than was needed when younger, a sensible diet, not too high
in protein and easily digested, and adequate but not
excessive exercise. You may find, with a Rott living in the
house, that old age weakens the bladder and the need to trot
outside becomes more frequent.

While everyone will urge you not to let your Rottweiler
become too fat, and this is certainly good advice in early and
middle age, you will find that Rotts, like humans, vary in the
amount of weight they carry. Some will become plump on a
very small food intake, others will eat all they can and
remain slim. As your Rott gets older do not worry too much
about this. If his tummy is one of the delights of old age then
let him enjoy it, provided he is still active and fit.

Old age can bring a loss of hearing and of sense of smell
and poor eyesight, although we have seen little signs of this
in our Rotts. When your Rott fails to come when called do
not immediately assume he is getting awkward in his old age.
It may very well be because he cannot hear or scent you as
well as in the past.

Be patient with your pensioners, treasure them and do not
be afraid to give them treats and privileges that would have
been denied to a younger dog.

Death

It is a sad fact that a dog's life is so much shorter than ours. It is a lucky owner whose loved companion of many years slips away while asleep in his bed by the fire having been fit and happy up to the last moment. On far too many occasions the decision has to be made by the owner. Nature sometimes lets the dog linger on too long in pain and incapacity. We have tried to show in this book the pride, courage and dignity of the Rottweiler. You are doing your dog no favours if you allow him to struggle on when he is no longer in control of his body or possibly of his mind. The last kindness that you can give your Rottweiler is a peaceful end to his life in the security of his own home and in his owner's arms. Failure to do so is not for love of your dog, it is a lack of courage on your part and is putting your feelings before those of the dog. Any able vet can give a sedative, followed by a lethal injection, in such a way that the dog slips quietly into sleep without distress or pain. The dog, unlike a human, is totally unaware of what is going to happen, unless you allow him to be dragged away by a strange person into a strange place. Have it done in his own home if at all possible and with you by his side. If you do not have the courage to be with your Rott at the end, calming and comforting him, then you do not deserve the years of devotion the Rott has given you.

You are left with one final duty. While your vet will probably agree to dispose of the body, such arrangements often leave much to be desired. Burial in your garden is not always possible. There are a number of pet crematoriums which will, if you so desire, arrange a separate cremation for your dog and, if you wish, return the ashes to you to be scattered in his favourite corner of the garden. The one where, as a puppy, he used to dig up your rose bushes.

If reading the last paragraphs has depressed you as much as it did us when we wrote them, there is one consolation you may have if you have bred from your Rott. When you return from saying goodbye to the old one you may, if you are lucky, have at your feet a son, or perhaps a granddaughter, who will give you the same happiness. Do not expect the youngster to be exactly the same as the old one. He or she will be an individual as all Rotts are, but you will find the same essential characteristics which made you love your first.

Nothing that we have said in this chapter on the possible ills of your Rottweiler should be construed as suggesting that you should not call in your vet in all cases of serious illness, and even for what appear to be minor ailments, if they persist. Learn to recognize symptoms and how to describe them. Early treatment can often save your dog from what otherwise could be serious illness. Your vet will take an interest in your dogs, be pleased when they are successful and commiserate when things go wrong. He is in a position to update his knowledge of veterinary medicine constantly and can often make helpful suggestions to you on aspects of management and maintaining good health. He will be aware of any canine epidemics in your area and able to advise on immunization against them. Help him by being aware of his problems, as well as expecting him to be aware of yours.

12

The Breed Standard

The Standard of a breed is drawn up by the relevant breed clubs and amended, approved and published by the Kennel Club. It is the written specification for the perfect dog. The Standard is the ideal which all breeders should aim for and by which all judging should be carried out. Breeders should constantly strive to breed as near as possible to the Standard and should not try to alter or interpret it to fit the animals they have produced.

Try as one may, it is not possible to reduce the description of a dog to a precise list of requirements supported by measurements, drawings, colour charts etc. It has to remain a written description, a word picture, aiming to create in the mind of the reader an image of the Rottweiler as we would like to see him.

While we would never claim that the Rottweiler Standard has ever been a literary masterpiece, we do consider that the 1986 Kennel Club Standard on which this chapter is based, has, by virtue of the removal of surplus words, standardization of layout and a rather brusque and efficient approach, lost any claim to paint a picture. Instead of a warm-hearted portrait, composed by lovers of the breed, we have a passionless list of desirable ingredients compiled by people with little knowledge or understanding of the Rottweiler. To be fair it does list the Rottweiler's desirable characteristics although in a very cold-blooded form.

We also take exception to a tendency to describe various external aspects of the dog by reference to the skeletal terminology when a perfectly satisfactory term, understood by all, exists in topographical anatomy. Furthermore, this practice is not consistent throughout the Standard.

Neither are we happy with various attempts that have been made to produce illustrated standards. While it may be argued that an illustration is more readily understood than a written description, a failure by the artist to illustrate a detail correctly can create a long-lasting error which will have far more effect than a misinterpretation of a written description by one person.

Show six artists the same landscape and you will get six different pictures. Show a breed standard to six different breeders and you will find six different interpretations of what it says. Not all of these variations will be disagreements as to what the standard requires. Some will arise from a breeder's inability to achieve, with the stock available to him, what the standard demands. This can lead to an attempt to alter the interpretation of the standard or even to a suggestion that the standard should be changed.

You should be aware how the Breed Standard came into existence. People who used the Rottweiler to help them with their daily work developed those qualities which fulfilled their purpose. They had no standard to use as a blue print but did have the far greater incentive of creating a dog for their needs. Only when the breed type was established did the breed clubs codify its desirable characteristics and produce the Breed Standard. Any attempt to interpret the Breed Standard, or to assess a dog against it, should always be made with the original function of the dog in mind.

If you look back at Chapter 1, 'Origin and Development of the Rottweiler', you will see that another influence is brought to bear on the appearance of the dog as described in the Standard. This is the wish by breeders aiming primarily for the show ring to clean up and improve the appearance of the breed. This desire should not be seized on by those who dislike the show ring as evidence that 'show breeders' ruin a breed. In fact show breeders are usually extremely conscientious in their wish to ensure that the breed retains its 'fitness for purpose', even at times to the extent of exaggerating to an unacceptable degree a feature of the breed which is considered desirable by those using the dog in the way it was originally intended to be used. We do not, however, consider that this has happened with Rottweilers. As we have said in Chapter 3, 'The Rottweiler in Great Britain', great care was taken to ensure that the Standard did not describe as desirable any characteristics which, if exaggerated, could act to the detriment of the dog. Further pressure to change a breed comes from the demand by the dog owning public and from some judges and exhibitors that its temperament should be changed, probably to make it a softer, more easy-going dog. There has been this pressure on Rottweilers and we consider it should be resisted. The desire to reduce all breeds to the common level of soft, cuddly, loveable and submissive household pets has already destroyed the true character of many breeds. Much of the appeal of the Rottweiler, not only to breeders but to the general public, is his tough, courageous spirit and his willingness to defend his owner and their property.

Breeders and judges vary in their interpretation of the Standard and place different values on the various faults and virtues. As a result of this we have what is known as 'type'. A dog may be described as the type produced or admired by a particular person. Alternatively it may be described as 'not his type'. There is nothing wrong with this. If all judges thought the same way the same dog would win all the time. Even more important, this variation of interpretation means that the overall quality is maintained and no single aspect of the breed is given undue emphasis.

We propose to study the Rottweiler Standard by taking each section in turn and giving our interpretation of its requirements. The relevant section of the Standard will be given first followed by our comments.

General Appearance
Above average size, stalwart dog. Correctly proportioned, compact and powerful form, permitting great strength, manoeuvrability and endurance.

What size is average? Probably Boxers and Labradors are best described as average; therefore the Rottweiler must be larger than both these breeds. The term 'above average size' is intended to give a quick indication of size by comparison and must not be interpreted as a desire for size for its own sake. Big is not necessarily beautiful and the laid-down measurements must always be kept in mind when considering size. Excessive size can lead to a clumsy, cloddy dog whose powers of endurance and manoeuvrability will be greatly curtailed. The aim is for a dog fast and agile enough to catch its quarry and heavy and strong enough to knock it down and hold it when caught.

The dictionary definition of 'stalwart' is strong, sturdy, dependable and courageous, which seems a perfect description of the Rottweiler.

'Correctly proportioned' is a phrase that can have many interpretations. To understand it one needs to have in one's mind the total description of the Rottweiler and its purpose. Balanced is a word used by many people when discussing the proportions of their ideal Rottweiler. Whether you talk of proportions or balance it is virtually an instinctive feeling that the dog is right, or wrong, as the case may be. Balance must be considered in conjunction with the next phrase, 'compact and powerful form'. Again using the dictionary definition compact gives us 'neatly fitted into a confined space' and 'solid, firm'. Compact is sometimes used in dog parlance to describe a square dog. Attractive as it may appear to some eyes, the Rott should not be square, although he should be very nearly so, as you will see in the section on Body. We are not, however, looking for a long willowy dog; rather a well co-ordinated powerhouse of bone and muscle.

The last phrase in this section, 'permitting great strength, manoeuvrability and endurance', really sums up what is desired from the dog as a result of the requirements of the rest of this section. Again we would remind you that no one of these characteristics should be exaggerated to the detriment of any of the others.

While the standard does not say so, there are and should be marked differences between the general appearance of dogs and bitches. These differences are not merely those of sex and height. Males should be larger overall, heavier-boned and more masculine in appearance. Bitches should look feminine and be lighter in bone and finer in head. It should be possible to tell the sex of a Rottweiler when standing in front of it. Remember that a large bitch can still show these feminine characteristics, and that femininity is not just a question of being small and petite. A 'doggy' bitch is just as undesirable as a 'bitchy' dog.

Characteristics
Appearance displays boldness and courage. Self-assured and fearless. Calm gaze should indicate good humour.

This section requires that the appearance of the Rottweiler should manifest qualities which are of the spirit rather than of the body. However, one look at a Rottweiler of the right type will show you that he or she does in fact display boldness, courage, self-assurance and fearlessness in a manner which makes these qualities visible to the eye. The original UK standard used the word bearing and in our opinion this gives a better picture of what is desired. The second requirement of this section is for a calm gaze and good humour. The Rottweiler has a very expressive face. His expression should be friendly, fearless and confident.

Temperament
Good-natured, not nervous, aggressive or vicious, courageous, biddable, with natural guarding instincts.

We have covered in Chapter 2, 'Character – Temperament and Ability', those aspects which make up the Rottweiler temperament. When considering this as part of the Standard one must differentiate between the Rott's attitude to humans and to other dogs. Towards humans he is certainly good-natured and biddable and has natural guarding instincts. He is certainly courageous under all circumstances. As far as aggression is concerned he is certainly not what is sometimes described as a 'fear biter', attacking humans because he is afraid of them. He is, however, as we have said, a proud dog, prepared to defend his position in the world and he certainly has the determination to get in the first blow against anything which he considers a threat.

Head and Skull
Head medium length, skull broad between ears. Forehead moderately arched as seen from side. Occipital bone well developed but not conspicuous. Cheeks well boned and muscled but not prominent. Skin on head not loose, although it may form a moderate wrinkle when attentive.

Muzzle fairly deep with topline level, and length of muzzle in relation to distance from well-defined stop to occiput to be as 2 to 3. Nose well developed with proportionately large nostrils, always black.

The Rottweiler head should be broad, and therefore the width between the ears is most important. Seen from in front and above, the head should give the impression of a blunt-ended triangle. The topline of the skull between the ears should be almost flat with the fold of the ears extending this line. The moderate arch of the forehead means what it says. Bulging foreheads are as undesirable as shallow ones. The occipital bone is best described as the highest point at the back of the skull. The cheeks and zygomatic arch, which is the bony ridge running from the lower edge of the eye socket back to the opening of the ear canal, should reflect by their musculation the strength of the Rottweiler jaw and its biting power. Over-development of this aspect will give a heavy, coarse, Bull Mastiff type of head. Too little development gives a Dobermann type. The skin on the head should fit closely, without excessive wrinkle or folds of loose skin. The moderate wrinkle which is allowed when the dog is attentive should not be interpreted as encouraging wrinkle. It is merely a frown of concentration. A dry head is the term usually used. Excessive wrinkle around the eyes frequently indicates a tendency towards entropion. The term 'fairly deep muzzle' again asks that it should not be exaggerated, either as too heavy and coarse or sharp-pointed and snipey. The muzzle should be well filled in under the eyes, thus creating the blunt-ended triangle mentioned before. The level topline of the muzzle means that the dog should not have a Roman nose as is often seen, or, more rarely, the upturned tip to the nose. The stop, which is where the muzzle joins the skull, should be well defined but not so pronounced as to give a beetle-browed effect. Neither should the stop be shallow and dished. The comparative length of muzzle to skull, which often causes confusion, simply means that if the distance from the tip of the nose to the stop is 2 inches then the distance from stop to occiput should be 3 inches, both figures increasing in proportion.

There is considerable variation in incorrect Rottweiler head types. There are overlarge, round heads, usually with too much wrinkle and with a relatively small nose stuck in the middle of it: the teddy-bear type. Others resemble Labradors, while others are of the long-muzzled, narrow-skulled type.

Eyes
Medium size, almond shaped, dark brown in colour, light eye undesirable, eyelids close-fitting.

The demand in this section for a medium sized almond shaped eye with close-fitting eyelids is a typical example of the original purpose of the Rottweiler influencing the present day Standard. The almond shape and close-fitting eyelid help to protect the eyes from sun and dust, both very necessary for a dog intended to spend his day driving cattle along dusty roads. The close-fitting eyelid also lessens the chance of entropion. A loose lower eyelid, showing the red haw or conjunctival lining, apart from being extremely unattractive, exposes the eye to infection and increased tear flow. There is little evidence to indicate whether a light-coloured eye, such as yellow, affects the dog's vision. It probably does not. It is, however, a cosmetic fault which certainly detracts from the dog's appearance. Large round eyes also detract from the dog's appearance and, being more liable to damage, are undesirable on both counts.

Ears
Pendant, small in proportion rather than large, set high and wide apart, lying flat and close to cheek.

Ears make a tremendous difference to the appearance of the Rottweiler's head. Of the right size and correctly placed, they complement a good head. Carried sideways, or even worse, thrown back or 'flying', they alter the head and expression completely. The use of the word pendant is intended to indicate that the ears hang downwards rather than present a pricked or erect ear. They should not be extended to pendulous, that is, hanging down and swinging.

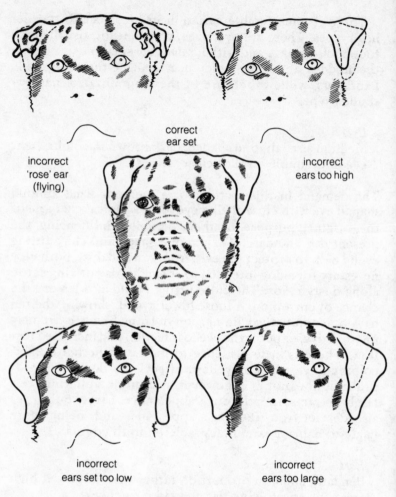

Figure 1 *Ears*

Pendulous does indeed describe some Rottweiler ears which, set too low on the skull and oversize, give their owners a most untypical appearance.

Mouth
Teeth strong, complete dentition with scissor bite, i.e. upper teeth closely overlapping the lower teeth and set square to the jaws. Flews black and firm, falling gradually

away towards corners of mouth, which do not protrude excessively.

The complete dentition asked for in this section, while desirable, should not be interpreted as absolutely essential. The lack of one or two pre-molars does not reduce the efficiency of the bite and missing pre-molars occur in examples of prehistoric dogs who obviously had a full and normal life. Fred Curnow quotes the case of a Dobermann who had one missing pre-molar in the lower jaw and one pre-molar too many in the upper jaw. It was ruled that as the dog had forty-two teeth its mouth was correct. He argued, and we would agree with him, that it had two mouth faults. Missing teeth are, in general, hereditary and this should be borne in mind when breeding. However, it is perfectly possible for a dog with missing teeth to produce large numbers of off-spring with complete dentition and as a fault, missing teeth should be weighed against the virtues of a particular dog.

The call for a scissor bite also requires careful consideration. A number of authorities point out that wild dogs, wolves, jackals and all other predatory animals have a pincer bite and that this is the most efficient bite for such animals.

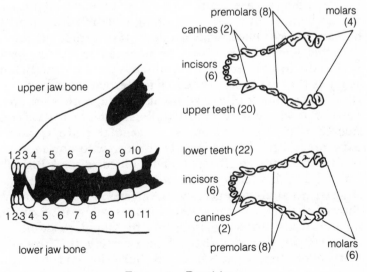

Figure 2 *Dentition*

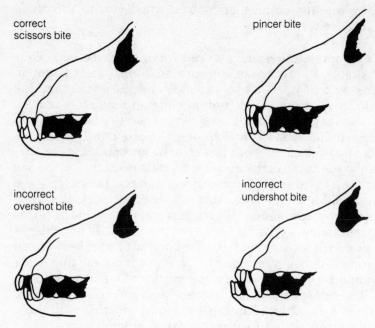

correct
scissors bite

pincer bite

incorrect
overshot bite

incorrect
undershot bite

Figure 3   *Bite*

In demanding a scissor bite, as do most breed standards, we are applying to our dogs something which is desirable for humans but not necessarily for dogs. It is further suggested that the demand for scissor, as opposed to pincer, leads eventually to an overshot bite, which is certainly inefficient as far as the dog is concerned. The German Standard does state that a pincer bite is admissible though not desirable. Most of us who started in Rottweilers in the early days considered that a pincer bite was acceptable. In our own experience, Ch. Chesara Dark Inquisitor, who won a total of twelve challenge certificates, had a pincer bite. A big substantial dog, his teeth at the age of twelve, when he died, showed no signs of excessive wear and his size certainly showed that he had not suffered from malnutrition during his life. While not suggesting that the Standard should be changed, we consider that when assessing the bite of a Rottweiler, these aspects should be borne in mind and in our opinion a pincer bite is much more acceptable than an overshot bite. When applied to puppies, however, we would remind you that in general, although not always, the lower jaw grows more than the upper, with the result that a slightly overshot bite will normally finish as scissor.

Technically speaking the flews of a dog are the upper lips, but by common usage the word tends to apply to upper and lower lips as it does here. Apart from the need for them to be black they should be close-fitting along the side of the jaw, without unsightly drooping pockets. At the corners, where the upper and lower lips join, the fold so formed should not be obtrusive. Some judges extend the requirement for black flews to the colour of the gums. There is nothing in the Standard to justify this but we would agree that dark gums look more attractive.

Neck

Of fair length, strong, round and very muscular. Slightly arched, free from throatiness.

'Of fair length' is a rather indeterminate term, so look for a length that complements the rest of the dog. Moderate length might be a better description. A short 'bull' neck is usually found with an upright shoulder. A 'ewe' neck is one where the neck remains almost the same diameter for the whole of its length instead of broadening at the base. A clean, well-arched neck greatly improves the carriage of the head and adds that elusive element of quality to the dog. Throatiness is excessively loose skin on the neck. A small amount of this, while undesirable, is almost unavoidable in males.

Forequarters

Shoulders well laid back, long and sloping, elbows well let down, but not loose. Legs straight, muscular, with plenty of bone and substance. Pasterns sloping slightly forward.

The requirement for the shoulder to be well laid back can best be explained by reference to the skeletal drawing (page 153). The normal interpretation of a correctly laid back shoulder is that the scapular or shoulder blade should form a 90 degree angle with the humerus, or upper arm. You can

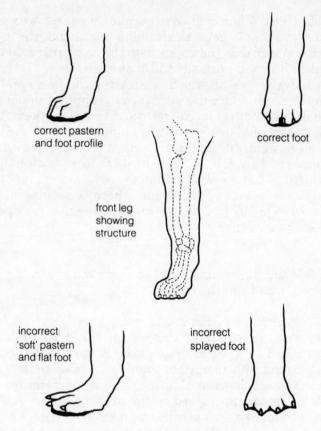

correct pastern
and foot profile

correct foot

front leg
showing
structure

incorrect
'soft' pastern
and flat foot

incorrect
splayed foot

Figure 4 *Front feet and pasterns*

measure it the other way round and say that the shoulder blade forms a 45 degree angle with a vertical line running through the shoulder joint.

While the shoulders should be muscular, an over-muscled shoulder, usually described as 'loaded in shoulder', will produce a bad front movement giving no room for the dog to stretch out, so that it paddles along with its elbows flying like wings. The demand for a straight front leg only applies as far down as the pastern, which should slope slightly forward. This is important, as the slight slope allows the shock of impact when running or jumping to be absorbed.

Body

Chest roomy, broad and deep with well-sprung ribs. Depth of brisket will not be more and not much less than 50 per cent of shoulder height. Back straight, strong and not too long, ratio of shoulder height to length of body should be as 9 is to 10, loins short, strong and deep, flanks not tucked up. Croup of proportionate length, and broad, very slightly sloping.

It is essential that the chest be broad and deep in a working dog. The word 'brisket' is a synonym for the sternum or breastbone but is used here to indicate a deep chest. Therefore the request that the depth of brisket be not more than and not much less than 50 per cent of shoulder height applies to the distance from withers to breastbone in relation to the dog's total height at the withers. Failure to stay close to these measurements will result in either a tall, leggy dog, or one which is squat and short in the leg. For the purpose of description in the Standard, the back of a dog is from just behind the withers to the hip bones. From the hip bones

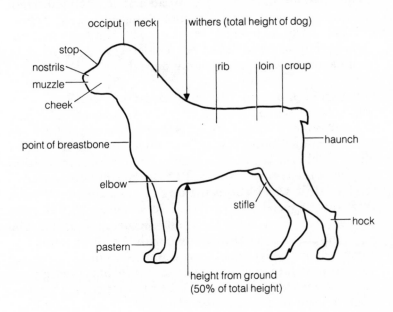

Figure 5 *Outline*

to the root of the tail it is the croup. The desired straight
back therefore means that the topline from withers to croup
is level and a straight line. The back should not be too short.
The Rottweiler should be just a little longer than he is tall.
Too long in the back makes the dog look weak. The ribs
should extend well back so that the loin is short. The short
loin adds to the Rottweiler's almost level underline, which is
virtually parallel with the topline. The tucked-up flanks
found in some Rottweilers are incorrect and destroy that
short-coupled appearance which is so desirable. However,
the Rottweiler is not a square dog. There is a tendency to
consider squareness, especially in males, as being desirable.
This is incorrect and the laid-down ratio of shoulder-height
to body-length should always be kept in mind. The vital
words in the description of the croup are 'very slightly
sloping'. An excessively sloping croup gives the rear end a
droopy drawers appearance. A croup that is too short and
level gives a high tail-set and a terrier outline.

Hindquarters

Upper thigh not too short, broad and strongly muscled.
Lower thigh well muscled at top, strong and sinewy below.
Stifles fairly well bent. Hocks well angulated without
exaggeration, metatarsals not completely vertical. Strength
and soundness of hock highly desirable.

Once again please refer to the skeletal drawing. The upper
thigh comprises the muscle groups surrounding the femur
or thigh bone. The lower thigh is the muscle region between
stifle and hock joint. The stifle or knee joint requires to be
fairly well bent. We do not want excessive hind angulation
as seen in the German Shepherd Dog. Neither do we want a
straight stifle which spoils the dog's stride. Broad, muscled
thighs are a special feature of the Rottweiler and the muscles
should be clearly visible, especially on the upper thigh. The
hock should form a definite angle with the lower thigh. For
some reason the Kennel Club committee which edited the
current Standard decided to get rather technical with their
use of the word metatarsals. To most dog people the word
hock is used to describe the whole of the lower leg from
hock joint to foot, and as with the front pastern the slight

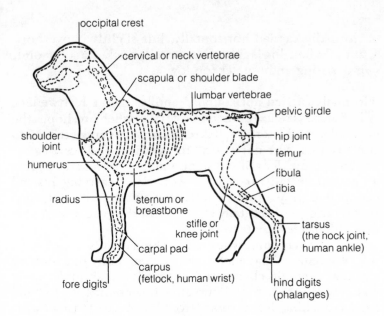

Figure 6 *Skeleton*

slope forward, described as not completely vertical, is intended to absorb shock.

Feet
Strong, round and compact with toes well arched. Hind feet somewhat longer than front. Pads very hard, toenails short, dark and strong. Rear dewclaws removed.

'Cat-like' probably best describes the desired foot of the Rottweiler. Short toe nails come from the correctly shaped foot and no amount of nail clipping will compensate for a badly shaped foot. Most people remove the front dewclaws, firstly because if left on they are easily caught and torn, and secondly because this gives a clean line to the leg. The Standard asks for rear dewclaws to be removed. Many Rottweilers are born without rear dewclaws and they can be eliminated to a great extent by selective breeding. Some breeders, ourselves included, prefer not to breed from Rottweilers who are born with hind dewclaws, believing that their presence tends to produce a cow-hocked dog.

Tail
Normally carried horizontally, but slightly above horizontal when dog is alert. Customarily docked at first joint, it is strong and not set too low.

'Normally carried horizontally' applies to the Rottweiler's tail when he is relaxed. In the show ring, when one hopes the dog is alert and attentive, it is reasonable to expect the tail to rise towards, but not reach, the vertical. Tail carriage is linked to croup length and slope and the correct croup gives an attractive tail carriage. A Rottweiler carrying his tail clamped tightly down is not only unattractive but also reveals a dog which totally fails to show the qualities listed as desirable under Characteristics.

The time may come when the docking of tails is banned by law. We believe that such a ban is completely unnecessary and that it would change the Rottweiler in an undesirable way. However, without pursuing the arguments for and against docking, it is necessary for breeders to consider what type of tail and tail carriage would be desirable if the Rottweiler were not docked. Our only written guidance in

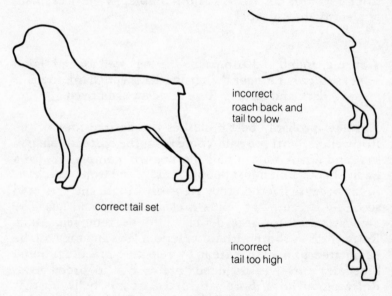

incorrect
roach back and
tail too low

correct tail set

incorrect
tail too high

Figure 7   *Back and tail set*

this decision is the 1901 Standard given in Appendix A. This calls for a strong, medium-length tail carried high, set at a steep angle. Present-day Rottweilers who have not been docked show variations in tail carriage, from one that is carried high and curled over the back to one carried low and hanging down to the hocks. The low-carried tail usually seems to come with a long and excessively sloping croup. The high-carried tail is usually found on Rottweilers with the type of hindquarters and croup which are considered desirable. It would, therefore, appear that if tails had to be left undocked it would be necessary to select the high-carried tail in order to preserve the desired conformation of the Rottweiler.

Gait/Movement

Conveys an impression of supple strength, endurance and purpose. While back remains firm and stable there is a powerful hindthrust and good stride. First and foremost, movement should be harmonious, positive and un-restricted.

In movement, the Standard once again demands that the appearance of the Rottweiler shall give the impression of qualities which are of the spirit rather than physical. Endurance is implied by the whole build and manner of the dog. Purpose is obvious to anyone who has seen a good Rott move. The dog knows where he is going and is determined to get there.

One of the dictionary definitions of supple is 'showing easy and graceful movement', and this word must, when applied to the Rottweiler, be used in conjunction with the next word, strength. It must not be interpreted as pliant, elegant or willowy.

The demand for the back to remain firm and stable is important. The level, straight back, asked for in the section on Body, should be retained when the dog moves. Many Rottweilers, even when apparently showing a level topline when standing, will lose it when moving. The back starts to undulate and the whole body starts to roll. The powerful hindthrust of a Rottweiler is most desirable and plays a major part not only in driving the dog forwards but in giving

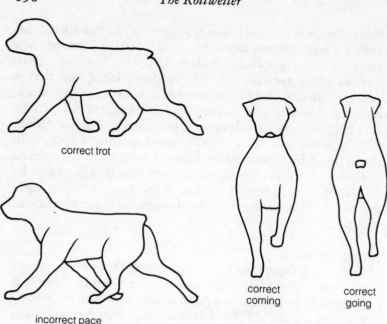

correct trot

incorrect pace

correct coming

correct going

Figure 8   *Gait*

the impression of purpose discussed above. The good stride means that the front legs should move well forward with the hind legs following through with good thrust from the hocks, covering as much ground as possible, without loss of ground coverage by an exaggerated lift of feet and pasterns. A high-stepping or 'Hackney' gait caused by steep shoulder angulation and upright pasterns is wasteful of energy and reduces endurance. This is another example of the Standard preserving the original purpose of the Rottweiler as a dog capable of maintaining a steady trot over long distances when driving cattle.

The final important word in this section is harmonious. Rottweiler experts have argued about the use of this word with its usual association with music. However, it does well describe the desirable Rottweiler movement with all parts moving in a compatible and co-ordinated whole.

This section of the Standard makes no mention of fore and aft movement, although the requirement in the section on Forequarters would seem to suggest that the front legs

Ch. Chesara Akilles, sire of 10 champions

Akilles clearing the 6-foot scale. (He should *not* be wearing a choke chain) *(Sally Anne Thompson)*

International and Nordic Champion Fandango's Fair Boy, sire of Ch. Chesara Akilles

Feeding time

Rottweilers are good with children (*Sally Anne Thompson*)

Ch. Chesara Dark Julia *(Diane Pearce)*

Ch. Chesara Dark Charles, dominant sire of the 1980s *(Diane Pearce)*

'Stalwart and courageous' – a group of Mrs Ann Wallet's Poirot Rottweilers
(Diane Pearce)

seen from in front should remain straight and parallel when moving. Judges tend to desire this type of movement and the occasional dog who does keep both front legs parallel is praised. However, a dog moving towards you will, as the weight comes off each leg, tend to move that leg in slightly towards the centre line and such movement is not only acceptable but anatomically correct. This does not mean that it is acceptable for the dog to single track, be out at elbows, toe in or out, or cross the front legs when moving; neither should he move wide in front. The same slight incline towards the centre line will be found with the back legs but again it is wrong if the legs move too close together, are cow-hocked, or move wider behind, i.e. are bandy. The other common fault in fore and aft movement is 'crabbing', when the fore and aft line of the dog's body does not move parallel with the direction of movement.

Coat

Which consists of top coat and undercoat, should be of medium length, coarse and flat. Undercoat essential on the neck and thighs, should not show through the outer coat. The hair may also be a little longer on the back of the forelegs and breachings.

The Rottweiler coat is designed to keep him both warm and dry. The medium length, coarse top coat should be weather proof and water resistant. It should feel harsh to the touch and the thin Dobermann coat is a fault. With a dog in good condition the coat should be glossy but not with the supple, glossy look that one finds in the Dobermann. Equally wrong is a soft, wavy, curly or long coat. The coat should lie flat, although some Rotts will show a slight wave at certain stages of coat growth. Long coats, that is of several inches in length, soft in texture and wavy, occur occasionally in Rottweilers. This is a major fault although one which selective breeding can quickly reduce to minimal proportions. The first sign of a long coat is usually seen in puppies from about six weeks of age when tufts of hair start to grow on the ends of the ears and the backs of the legs. The undercoat may be black, grey or fawn, the first two being the more common. The black undercoat is difficult to see because of the black topcoat. The grey or fawn undercoat tends to grow thicker than the black and will become visible during a moult when the top coat (guard hairs) have become thin. While the Standard requires that the undercoat should not show through the top coat, this is unavoidable at some stages of moulting. Most judges accept this temporary visibility and in fact consider that it gives conclusive proof of the presence of the undercoat. Rottweilers living in hot climates will very sensibly shed most of their undercoat and the top coat may become thinner.

Colour

Black with clearly defined markings as follows: a spot over each eye, on cheeks as a strip around each side of muzzle, but not on bridge of nose, on throat, two clear triangles on either side of the breast bone, on forelegs from carpus downward to toes, on inside of rear legs from hock to toes, but not completely eliminating black from back of legs, under tail. Colour of markings from rich tan to mahogany and should not exceed 10 per cent of body colour. White marking is highly undesirable. Black pencil markings on toes is desirable. Undercoat is grey, fawn, or black.

This paragraph, in attempting to define in detail the position of the tan markings, does in fact create confusion over an aspect of the Rottweiler which in the past was quite clear to anyone who knew dogs of the black and tan breeds, of which there are many. It is an odd genetic fact that any black and tan breed has the tan markings in exactly the same positions. However, if you study the requirements of the Standard carefully it will tell you the location of the tan. The carpus is the joint between the forearm and the pastern and the tan on the front legs should, therefore, cover what we know as the pastern down to the toes. It can, and frequently does, run a little higher up the foreleg.

The main rules when assessing tan markings are that they should be clearly defined, that there should be no sooty or dark patches within the tan area, that the various areas should be completely separate and not run into each other, that they should not come too high up the outside of the legs and should not extend to the flanks and brisket. The requirement that the tan markings should not exceed 10 per cent of body colour can only be considered a rough guide, and the thought of an over-enthusiastic judge armed with ruler, calculator and reams of paper, triumphantly establishing that the tan areas of a particular dog total over 10 per cent, is too ludicrous to contemplate. Your eye, instinct and the rules we have given you will soon tell you whether the tan areas are acceptable or not. We would remind you that although the Standard gives a maximum area of tan it lays down no minimum and, in our opinion, lack of tan markings is as undesirable as an excess of tan.

The colour of the tan, 'from rich tan to mahogany', needs consideration. Most people consider mahogany to be the most attractive but we must admit that this colour can have a tendency to sootiness. At the other extreme, a very pale tan is undesirable. This colour often goes with excessively large areas of tan and can give a false impression of the outline of the dog.

Very rarely white markings will occur in places other than the chest. We have seen examples of a white foot and a white patch on the muzzle. As we have said, these are very rare but must be considered a major fault. The tiny patch of white hairs on the chest occurs much more frequently. This usually fades into the tan by maturity and unless it persists as a solid patch of white, should be considered a very minor fault.

Size

Dogs' height at shoulder between 63–69 cms (25–27 ins). Bitches between 58–63.5 cms (23–25 ins). Height should always be considered in relation to general appearance.

These figures are clear and need little explanation. Height should always be considered in conjunction with the relative measurements given in the section on Body. A dog of 27 ins at the shoulder whose depth of brisket is only, say, 11 ins, is obviously wrong, as is the dog measuring 25 ins whose depth of brisket is 15 ins. Furthermore, the ratio of height to length of 9 as to 10 means that a 27 ins dog should have a body length of 30 ins.

Faults

Any departure from the foregoing points should be considered a fault and the seriousness with which the fault should be regarded should be in exact proportion to its degree.

Unlike standards issued in other countries, the Kennel Club does not allow what are called disqualifying faults to be listed in the Standard. It follows that while a judge may reject and not place a dog with a particular fault, the judge is not under an arbitrary instruction to disqualify the dog because of certain faults. It is considered that any fault should be balanced against the overall quality of the dog and it is at the judge's discretion as to what weight should be given to a particular fault. This does mean that some judges will penalize a dog more heavily than other judges for a particular fault.

The term 'fault judging' is used when a judge rejects a dog for a particular fault, without taking into account his virtues, which may be many. Fault judging is sometimes used by inexperienced judges as providing an easy reason for rejecting dogs for faults which are obvious to even an untrained eye. Examples are missing teeth, eye colour or lack of tan markings.

Note

Male animals should have two apparently normal testicles fully descended into the scrotum.

The term used to describe a male with two apparently normal testicles fully descended is 'entire'. Failure to have both testicles descended is, therefore, described as 'not entire'. You will also hear the term 'unilateral cryptorchid' used to describe a male with only one testicle descended and 'bilateral cryptorchid' when neither have descended.

This, then, is the Rottweiler Standard and our interpretation of it. Obviously those aspects which could affect the dog's health and ability to lead a normal life are more important than those which are largely cosmetic. However, if you intend to play your part in the future of the Rottweiler you must, in making decisions based on the Standard, whether when breeding or judging, take all the breed's features into account.

We also hope to have given you an understanding of the way in which the Rottweiler's original purpose has influenced the requirements of the Standard.

Appendix A
The First Rottweiler Breed Standard, 1901

The first known standard was laid down by Albert Kull in 1883 for the International Club for Leonberger and Rottweiler Dogs at Stuttgart. This was published in 1901.

This first standard ran as follows:

General Appearance Medium to large, strong-boned, robust figure, square-built, seeming short rather than too long. Bitch always smaller and longer in the back.

Head Skull broad and well-arched with well-marked frontal depression. Short muzzle, bridge of nose broad, ample flews with corners of mouth moderately prominent, cheeks full and round. Eyes medium-sized, full with fiery and intelligent expression, invariably dark brown. Medium to small high-set ears widely separated by the broad skull, placed forward in the alert position, otherwise lying back. Broad nose with wide nostrils, invariably black. The whole head quite dry without any surplus skin.

Neck Short, powerfully muscled, passing into the shoulders with strongly arched nape, dry and without dewlaps.

Forequarters Shoulders steep and long, well-set. Upper arm short, muscular and set close to the chest. Forelegs well-muscled and sinewy, straight when viewed from all sides, with elbows lying well under the chest. Pasterns short, broad, with strong bones and sinews, paws hard and tight, toes well-arched with strong nails.

Trunk Ribcage elliptical, well-developed, ribs deep and well-sprung. Back short, compact and completely straight with short, very powerful kidney region, looking very broad and flat when seen from above. Belly only slightly drawn up, buttocks short with high-set tail and firm muscle-pad.

Hindquarters Steep with high hocks. Upper part of leg long with unusually powerful and muscular thighs. Lower part of leg short with prominent muscles and sinews. Achilles tendon well-developed. Metatarsus long, toes tight and less arched than the front ones.

Tail The dog is often born with a stumpy tail and this is always preferred; otherwise strong, of medium length, well covered with hair and carried high and at a steep angle.

Colour Preferably and most commonly black with russet or yellow markings over the eyes, at the lips and on the inner and under side of the legs as well as on the bottom. Alternatively black stripes on an ash-grey background with yellow markings, plain red with black nose, or dark wolf-grey with black head and saddle, but always with yellow markings. White markings on the chest and legs occur very frequently and are admissible if they are not too extensive.

Coat Unusually thick with strong undercoat, the hairs firm, straight and reasonably long, wiry and hard, the whole coat very abundant, thick and weatherproof, and having, where black, a velvety sheen.

Faults Head and body too long and narrow, flews and corners of the mouth too pendulous, wrinkled face, light eyes and nose, ears set too deep or large, weak bones, flabby muscles, soft or spreading toes, coat scanty or lifeless, or too long and soft.

Qualities With a quiet, good-natured character and measured and deliberate movement he combines exceptional courage, endurance and energy. He is excellent and agreeable as a companion, and heedless of weather and incorruptible as a watch-dog, performing his duties carefully but without unnecessary noise.

Appendix B

Breed Champions up to 31 December 1986

* IMPORT

Name	Sex	Birth	Sire	Dam	Breeder	Owner
Chesara Dark Destiny	B	10.6.64	Rintelna The Bombardier C.D. ex., U.D.ex.	Chesara Portlaynum Bridgitte	Mrs J. Elsden	Mrs J. Elsden
* Chesara Luther	D	22.2.64	Ch. Baldur v. Habenichts	Astrida	M. Meijerink	Mrs J. Elsden
Erich of Mallion	D	23.5.60	Rudi Eulenspiegel of Mallion	Quinta Eulenspiegel of Mallion	Mrs J. Chadwick	Miss E. Cook
Chesara Dark Soliloquy	B	16.5.65	Ch. Chesara Luther	Chesara Portlaynum Bridgitte	Mrs J. Elsden	Mrs J. Elsden
Horst from Blackforest C.D.ex.	D	25.1.66	Rintelna The Bombardier C.D. ex., U.D.ex.	Anouk from Blackforest	Mrs M. Macphail	Mrs M. Macphail
Hildegard from Blackforest	B	25.1.66	Rintelna The Bombardier C.D.ex., U.D.ex.	Anouk from Blackforest	Mrs M. Macphail	Miss E. Harrap
* Chesara Akilles	D	6.6.66	Int. & Nordic Ch. Fandangos Fair Boy	Dackes Ina	R. Hamberg	Mrs J. Elsden

Name	Sex	Birth	Sire	Dam	Breeder	Owner
Chesara Dark Opal	B	24.10.66	Ch. Chesara Luther	Chesara Portlaynum Bridgitte	Mrs J. Elsden	Miss G. Ogilvy-Shepherd
* Ero v. Bucheneck	D	5.12.66	Emir v. Freienhagen	Indra v. Schloss Westerwinkel	H. Plogmann	J. Baldwin
Chesara Dark Inquisitor	D	25.12.66	Ch. Chesara Luther	Ch. Chesara Dark Destiny	Mrs J. Elsden	Mrs J. Elsden
Retsacnals Gamegards Gallant Attempt	D	15.9.67	Ch. Horst from Blackforest C.D.ex.	Blanka v. Ostertal	Mrs V. McLean	Mrs W. Boyd
Portia Moriconium	B	28.9.67	Ch. Chesara Luther	Edda von Mark	Miss E. Ollivant	B. Birke
Bhaluk Princess Birgitta	B	30.6.68	Ch. Ero v. Bucheneck	Elsa from Blackforest	Mrs C. Joseph	Mrs C. Joseph
Chesara Dark Jasmin	B	11.7.68	Ch. Chesara Akilles	Chesara Dark Revelry	Mrs J. Hobbs	Mrs P. Lanz
Chesara Dark Gossip	B	13.9.68	Ch. Chesara Akilles	Chesara Dark Memory	Mrs J. Elsden	Mrs J. Elsden
Chesara Dark Kruger	D	25.6.69	Ch. Chesara Akilles	Chesara Lenlee Ophelia	Mrs D. Skinner	Mrs J. Elsden
Borgvaale Bonita	B	30.3.70	Ch. Chesara Akilles	Chesara Dark Intuition	Mrs P. Lanz	Mrs P. Lanz

Name	Sex	Date	Sire	Dam	Breeder	Owner
Borgvaale Balthazar	D	30.3.70	Ch. Chesara Akilles	Chesara Dark Intuition	Mrs P. Lanz	S. Pierre
Jentris Gerontius	D	23.4.70	Gamegards Lars V.D. Hobertsberg	Chesara Dark Revelry	Mrs J. Hobbs	Mrs J. Hobbs
Chedi Bonnie of Cenlea	B	28.4.70	Ch. Chesara Akilles	Byxfield Sampanda	C. Nash	Mrs C. Cameron
* Gamegards Bulli V.D. Waldachquelle	D	9.11.70	Bulli v. Hungerbuhl	Anka v. Reichenbachle	J. Kubler	Mrs J. Woodgate
Chesara Byxfield Akela	B	11.12.70	Ch. Chesara Akilles	Byxfield Anouk of Cenlea	Mrs E. Henbest	Mrs J. Elsden
Chesara Dark Warlord	D	15.9.71	Ch. Ero v. Bucheneck	Chesara Dark Katrin	Mrs J. Elsden	Mrs J. Elsden
Chesara Dark Pageant	B	13.1.72	Ch. Chesara Dark Kruger	Ch. Chesara Dark Gossip	Mrs J. Elsden	P. Radley
Robvale Max-I-Million	D	27.1.72	Ch. Chesara Akilles	Anna Delviento	Mrs S. Jeys	Mrs E. Davis
Dusky Victoria of Vaelune	B	15.2.72	Ch. Retsacnal Gamegards Gallant Attempt	Retsacnal Chesara Dark Zinnia	Mrs W. Boyd	Mrs D. Cording
Borgvaale Vonda	B	10.8.72	Ch. Jentris Gerontius	Ch. Borgvaale Bonita	Mrs P. Lanz	Mrs N. Simmons
Prince Gelert of Bhaluk	D	23.8.72	Ch. Gamegards Bulli V.D. Waldachquelle	Bhaluk Princess Delilah	Mrs P. Reeve	P. Gedge

Name	Sex	Birth	Sire	Dam	Breeder	Owner
* Castor of Intisari	D	5.12.72	Int.Ch. Farro V.H. Brabantpark	Danish Ch. Ursula	Mrs M. Jensen	P. Radley
Borgvaale Halla of Helvetia	B	20.1.73	Ch. Chesara Akilles	Chesara Dark Intuition	Mrs P. Lanz	Mrs P. Lanz
Chesara Dark Leila	B	15.3.73	Ch. Chesara Dark Kruger	Ch. Chesara Byxfield Akela	Mrs J. Elsden	W. Burrows
Schutz From Gamegards	B	10.4.73	Ch. Gamegards Bulli V.D. Waldachquelle	Lohteyn Loyalty	N. Brendon	Mrs J. Woodgate
Attila Briseis	D	15.9.73	Ch. Gamegards Bulli V.D. Waldachquelle	Attila Astrid	Mrs A. Bryant	Mrs A. Bryant
Borgvaale Lion City River of Ritonshay	D	25.12.73	Ch. Jentris Gerontius	Ch. Borgvaale Bonita	Mrs P. Lanz	Mrs R. Parratt
Byxfield Demretis of Herburger	D	12.1.74	Ch. Chesara Akilles	Byxfield Anouk of Cenlea	Mrs E. Henbest	Mrs R. Bowring
* Ausscot Hasso v. Marchenwald	D	15.3.74	Int.Ch. Elko.v. Kastanienbaum	Cora v. Reichenbachle	Herr Gallas	G. McNeill
Casses Lass of Potterspride	B	1.6.74	Ch. Prince Gelert of Bhaluk	Aarons Pugue	H. Ward	Mrs V. Slade
Vaelune Alexis	D	5.7.74	Brooklow Coligua	Ch. Dusky Victoria of Vaelune	Mrs D. Cording	Mrs D. Cording

Name	Sex	Date	Sire	Dam	Breeder	Owner
Whitebeck Touch Wood	D	10.7.74	Ch. Gamegards Bulli V.D. Waldachquelle	Wandrin Shadow of Whitebeck	Miss E. Newell	Miss E. Newell
Janbicca The Superman	D	27.7.74	Ch. Gamegards Bulli V.D. Waldachquelle	Amy of Torside	Mrs K. Bloom	Mrs K. Bloom
Adoram Cordelia	B	16.11.74	Ch. Castor of Intisari	Adoram Horsa	M. Quinney	M. Quinney
Adoram Lennart	D	16.11.74	Ch. Castor of Intisari	Adoram Horsa	M. Quinney	P. Radley
Graefin Tansy Baronin	B	15.12.74	Nygra Night Watch	Jentris Ariadne	Mrs L. Burton	Mrs L. Burton
Princess Malka of Bhaluk	B	5.2.75	Ch. Gamegards Bulli V.D. Waldachquelle	Bhaluk Princess Demeter	Mrs B. Martin	Mrs B. Martin
GBOS Goshawk	D	26.2.75	Upend Gallant Alf	GBOS Gladeyes	Miss G. Ogilvy-Shepherd	Mrs C. Patterson
Poirot Camilla	B	21.8.75	Poirot Brigadier	Jentris Nicolina Belle	Mrs A. Wallett	Mrs A. Wallett
Chesara Dark Julia	B	12.9.75	Joris	Chesara Dark Laura	Mrs J. Elsden	Mrs J. Elsden
Javictreva Team Mascot of Panelma	B	16.9.75	Borgvaale Harlem Trotter of Ritonshay	Ch. Borgvaale Vonda	Mrs N. Simmons	Mrs P. Bryant
Upend Gallant Gairbert	D	15.4.76	Torro Triomfator From Chesara	Lucky Thirtry of Upend	Mrs B. Butler	Mrs B. Butler

Name	Sex	Birth	Sire	Dam	Breeder	Owner
Anelie of Basslaw	B	3.6.76	Ch. GBOS Goshawk	Chesara Dark Lola of Basslaw	Mrs A. Forsythe	Mrs A. Forsythe
Chesara Dark Roisterer	D	18.7.76	Torro Triomfator of Chesara	Borgvaale Venus	Mrs J. Adams	Mrs J. Elsden
Linguards Jupiter	D	23.7.76	Poirot Brigadier	Bassenthwaite Carol	Mrs M. Simpson	Mrs M. Simpson
Panevors Proud Kamille	B	28.8.76	Ch. Ausscot Hasso v. Marchenwald	Gamegards Zenith of Panevor	M. Hammond	M. Hammond
Panevors Proud Kinsman	D	28.8.76	Ch. Ausscot Hasso v. Marchenwald	Gamegards Zenith of Panevor	M. Hammond	M. Hammond
Jagen Dust My Blues	B	18.9.76	Ch. Castor of Intisari	Kenstaff Jaega	L. Price	P. Radley
Jagen Mr Blue	D	18.9.76	Ch. Castor of Intisari	Kenstaff Jaega	L. Price	J. Dalloway
Ronpaula Bold Avenger	D	15.10.76	Borgvaale Harlem Trotter of Ritonshay	Upend Gay Dilemma	R. Young	R. Young & G. Neilson
Herburger Count Ferro	D	9.11.76	Lord V.D. Grurmannsheide of Herburger	Rawtar Suco Emma of Herburger	Mrs R. Hughes	W. Bromley
Graefin Tamsley Witt	B	15.11.76	Nygra Night Watch	Jentris Ariadne	Mrs L. Burton	Mrs L. Burton

GBOS Gaytimes	B	21.11.76	Ch. Ausscot Hasso v. Marchenwald	GBOS Gladeyes	Mrs G. Ogilvy-Shepherd	Mrs H. Wilson
Fryerns Advocator	D	2.1.77	Ch. Janbicca The Superman	Breckley Christmas Rose	Mrs M. Nash	Mrs M. Nash
Ablaze of Janbicca	D	2.1.77	Ch. Janbicca The Superman	Breckley Christmas Rose	Mrs M. Nash	Mrs K. Bloom
Linguard Norge	D	21.6.77	Ch. Castor of Intisari	Poirot Crisandra	Mrs M. Simpson	J. Coleridge
Jagen Astrix	B	17.8.77	Poirot Brigadier	Kenstaff Jaega	L. Price	A. Davies
Isaela The Saxon	D	1.9.77	Ch. Janbicca The Superman	Nygra Night Solo	M. Heydon	G. Riches
Poirot Edwina	B	2.9.77	Chesara Dark Joris	Jentris Nicolina Belle	Mrs A. Wallett	Mrs A. Wallett
Nedraw Black Sunshine	B	26.2.78	Ch. Borgvaale Lion City River of Ritonshay	Borgvaale Sea Witch	F. Warden	Mrs & Miss Yates
Herburger Countess Natasha	B	28.10.78	Ch. Whitebeck Touch Wood	Rawtar Suco Emma of Herburger	Mrs R. Hughes	Mrs R. Hughes
Vaelune Denethor	D	16.11.78	Poirot Brigadier	Ch. Dusky Victoria of Vaelune	Mrs D. Cording	Mrs D. Cording
Ausscot Cover Girl	B	13.4.78	Ch. Ausscot Hasso v. Marchenwald	Linguards Jacqueline	G. McNeill	G. McNeill

Name	Sex	Birth	Sire	Dam	Breeder	Owner
Madason Dauntless	B	5.1.79	Ch. Borgvaale Lion City River of Ritonshay	Corda Buccaneer of Madason	Mrs M. Atkinson	Mrs M. Atkinson
Chesara Dark Hermina	B	21.1.79	Chesara Dark Herod	Chesara Dark Wilhelmina	Mrs J. Elsden	Mrs J. Elsden
Ausscot Donnerstag	D	15.3.79	Ch. Ausscot Hasso v. Marchenwald	Linguards Jacqueline	G. McNeill	G. McNeill
Nobane Bianka	B	17.4.79	Ch. Borgvaale Lion City River of Ritonshay	Bamber Portia	Mrs J. Ockenden	Mrs J. Ockenden
Karla of Heranmine	B	13.10.74	Arquebus By Knight	Lisanbrya Raincloud	Mrs M. Bennett	W. Bromley
Chesara Dark Charles	D	21.11.79	Chesara Dark Herod	Chesara Juliette von Mark	Mrs J. Elsden	Mrs J. Elsden
Panevors Proud Chicasaw	B	8.12.79	Ch. Panevors Proud Kinsman	Owlcroft Candida	M. Hammond	Mrs Goodwin
Rudi Anton Bali	D	8.12.79	Owlcroft Omega	Owlcroft Diana	Mr Ratcliffe	E. Woodward
Chesara Dark Hunters Dawn From Yorlander	B	24.1.81	Ch. Chesara Dark Charles	Chesara Dark Wilhelmina	Mrs J. Elsden	Mrs J. Elsden

Name		Date	Sire	Dam		
Jagen Blue Trigo	B	17.5.79	Poirot Brigadier	Jagen Reprint	L. Price	A. G. Broom
Panevors Proud Marksman of Jarot	D	28.5.79	Blackforest Meister Maik	Ch. Panevors Proud Kamille	M. Hammond	Mrs J. Anderson
Ausscot Franzell From Upend	B	25.1.80	Ch. Ausscot Hasso von Marchenwald	Ch. Ausscot Cover Girl	G. McNeill	Mrs B. Butler
Jagen Blue Aria	B	4.8.80	Ch. Janbicca The Superman	Jagen Midnight Blue	L. Price	L. Price
Janbicca Dear Dazzler of Torrento	B	23.9.80	Ch. Upend Gallant Gairbert	Dear Delinquent of Janbicca	Mrs J. Bloom	Mrs J. Knox
Pendley Goldfinch	D	27.9.80	Ch. Chesara Dark Roisterer	Ch. Nedraw Black Sunshine	Mrs J. Yates	Mrs T. Killick
Cuidado The Dandy	D	22.12.80	Poirot The Ferryman	Poirot Delilah of Cuidado	Mrs K. Wood	Mrs K. Wood
Dejavu Sweet Sensation	B	5.6.81	Ch. Chesara Dark Charles	Madason Beau Belle of Dejavu	Mrs J. Harper	Mrs J. Edwards
Caprido Operetta from Thewina	B	29.6.81	Ch. Chesara Dark Charles	Lyric from Caprido	Mrs D. Skinner	Mrs A. Garside-Neville
Caprido Minstrel of Potterspride	D	29.6.81	Ch. Chesara Dark Charles	Lyric from Caprido	Mrs D. Skinner	Mrs V. Slade
Herburger Touch of Brilliance from Vanhirsch	D	6.7.81	Phantom Herald of Herburger	Poirot Francesca of Herburger	Mrs R. Bowring	Mrs J. Heath

Name	Sex	Birth	Sire	Dam	Breeder	Owner
Rottsann Classic Crusader of Vormond	D	14.5.81	Chesara Dark Herod	Poirot Fantasia	Mrs C. Brady	Mrs J. Dunhill
Rottsann Classic Gold	B	14.5.81	Chesara Dark Herod	Poirot Fantasia	Mrs C. Brady	Mrs C. Brady
Panelma The Highwayman	D	25.9.81	Ch. Chesara Dark Charles	Panelma The Special Lady	Mrs M. Bryant	Mrs M. Bryant
Panelma The Adventurer	D	25.9.81	Ch. Chesara Dark Charles	Panelma The Special Lady	Mrs M. Bryant	Mrs M. Bryant
Upend Gay Quilla	B	2.12.81	Jagen Blue Andante	Christmas Carol of Upend	Mrs B. Butler	Mrs B. Butler
Rottsann Classic Centurion	D	14.5.81	Chesara Dark Herod	Poirot Fantasia	Mrs C. Brady	W. Bromley
Varenka Magic Madam	B	27.11.83	Varenka The Senator	Frybergs Bonafide	G. Rattray	G. Rattray
Chesara Dark Rachel	B	25.11.82	Ch. Chesara Dark Charles	Ch. Chesara Dark Julia	Mrs J. Elsden	Mrs J. Elsden
Varenka Rare Secret	B	4.8.82	Ch. Pendley Goldfinch	Frybergs Bonafide	G. Rattray	Mrs Hamilton
Poirot Led Zeppelin	D	18.8.82	Jannavic Alexis	Poirot Camilla	Mrs A. Wallett	Mrs Toes

Name	Sex	Date	Sire	Dam		
Lara Vorfelder Beauty at Lloydale	B	9.4.82	Jagen Blue Andante	Summerlyn Antoinette	Mrs K. Moreton	Mrs J. Thomas
Rich Bitch at Potterspride	B	8.3.83	Ch. Caprido Minstrel of Potterspride	Potterspride Bronze Angel	Mrs L. Shaw	Mrs V. Slade
Yorlanders Grecian Girl of Vonmark	B	8.9.83	Chesara Dark Herod	Chesara Dark Hunters Dawn from Yorlander	Mrs K. Hindley	Mrs J. Dunhill
Taroh Rowena at GBOS	B	4.9.83	GBOS Gillie	Taroh Tamarind	Mrs H. Wilson	Miss G. Ogilvy-Shepherd
Jagen Blue Dale	B	14.1.83	Ch. Chesara Dark Charles	Ch. Jagen Blue Aria	L. Price	L. Price
Glint of Gold at Erland	B	8.3.83	Ch. Caprido Minstrel of Potterspride	Potterspride Bronze Angel	Mrs L. Shaw	Mrs J. Trowbridge
Vanhirsch April Lord	D	12.4.83	Ch. Herburger Touch of Brilliance from Vanhirsch	Herburger Countess Lida of Vanhirsch	Mrs J. Heath	Mrs J. Heath
Chosin Circe	B	4.5.83	Madason Hurricane	Bamber Brenda of Chosin	C. E. James	Mrs M. Harris
Upend Gallant Theodoric	D	10.9.83	Ch. Caprido Minstrel of Potterspride	Upend Gay Jenny	Mrs B. Butler	Mrs B. Butler
Blue The Boy Wonder at Panelma	D	29.11.83	Zandawn Cerebus	Reit Mollie of Truestar	Mrs P. Bray	Mrs M. Bryant

Name	Sex	Birth	Sire	Dam	Breeder	Owner
Tellimar Victory at Heranmine	D	23.1.84	Ch. Rottsann Classic Crusader of Vormund	Chaymaie Louisianna from Tellimar	B. Mitchell	W. Bromley
Rottsann Regal Romance	B	1.4.84	Jagen Blue Andante	Rottsann Classic Crystal	Mrs C. Brady	Mrs E. Bland-Kerr
Aylsham Beauty of Potterspride	B	30.6.84	Ch.Caprido Minstrel of Potterspride	Poirot Katrina	Mrs Poole	Mrs V. Slade

Appendix C
Rottweiler Registration Totals
1965 to 1986

1965 –	8	1976 –	157
1966 –	48	1977 –	211
1967 –	101	1978 –	635
1968 –	122	1979 –	1033
1969 –	163	1980 –	1298
1970 –	164	1981 –	1641
1971 –	249	1982 –	2466
1972 –	263	1983 –	3526
1973 –	306	1984 –	4690
1974 –	332	1985 –	6836
1975 –	401	1986 –	8374

A change in the Kennel Club registration system during 1976 and 1977 resulted in a distortion of the figures for these years. In fact Rottweilers were steadily increasing during this period.

In 1986 the Rottweiler became the seventh most popular dog in the UK and the third most popular in the Working Group.

Appendix D
Glossary of German Terms

Short Glossary of German descriptive terms, useful when reading German reports or the pedigrees of imported dogs.

Abzeichen (A):	Markings
Ahnen:	Ancestors
Ahnentafel:	Pedigree
Allgemeine Erscheinung:	General appearance
Alter:	Age
Alterklasse (AK):	Adult class
Angekört:	Certified suitable for breeding
Augen:	Eyes
Ausdruck:	Character
Bauch:	Belly
Befriedigend (B):	Fair
Behaarung:	Coat
Belegt:	Bred
Besitzer:	Owner
Bewertung:	Qualification
Braun:	Brown
Breit:	Broad
Brust (Br):	Chest
Deckfarbe:	Predominant colour
Dunkel (D):	Dark
Ehrenpreis:	Prize of honour
Eltern:	Parents
Eng:	Narrow
Enkel, Enkelin:	Grandson, granddaughter
Erziehung:	Upbringing, training
Farbe:	Colour
Fassbeine:	Bow-legged
Fassrippe:	Barrel-ribbed
Flanke:	Loin
Fluchtig:	Fleet
Futterzustand:	Fine condition
Gang:	Gait
Gelb (G):	Gold

Geschleschtsgeprage:	Sex-quality
Gesundheit:	Sound health
Gewinkelt:	Angulated
Geworfen:	Whelped
Glatterhaarig:	Smooth-coated
Gross:	Large
Grosseltern:	Grandparents
Gut (G):	Good
Hals:	Throat, neck
Harmonisch:	Coordinated
Hart:	Hard
Hasenfuss:	Hare-foot(ed)
Hinterbeine:	Hindlegs
Hocke:	Hock
Hoden:	Testicles
Hohe:	Height
Hund:	Dog (applies to male and female)
Hundin (H):	Bitch
Jugend:	Youth
Jugendklasse (J.K):	Youth class
Junghund:	Puppy
Katzenfuss:	Catfoot
Kippohr:	Soft ear
Klein:	Small
Knocken:	Bones
Körbuch:	Stud book
Körzucht:	Good reproductive qualities
Kruppe:	Croup
Kurz:	Short
Lang:	Long
Länge:	Length
Langhaarig:	Long-coated
Muskeln:	Muscles
Mutter:	Dam
Nachschub:	Drive, thrust
Nagel:	Claw
Nase:	Nose
Oberarm:	Upper arm
Oberschlachtig:	Overshot
Ohren:	Ears
Pfote:	Paw
Rasse:	Breed
Rein:	Pure
Rot (R):	Red
Rippen:	Ribs

Rude (R):	Dog (as against bitch)
Rund:	Round
Rute:	Tail
Schädel:	Skull
Scheu:	Shy
Schulter:	Shoulder
Schulterblatt:	Shoulder blade
Schuss-scheu:	Gun-shy
Schussfest:	Gun-proof
Schwanz:	Tail
Schwarz:	Black
Stell:	Steep
Stockhaar:	Harsh coat
Tief:	Deep
Traben:	Trotting
Trocken:	Dry
Uberwinkelt:	Over-angulated
Ungenügend (O):	Poor
Unterschlachtig:	Undershot
Vater:	Sire
Verein:	Club
Verkaüflig (Verk):	For sale
Vorderbeine:	Forelegs
Vorderbrust:	Forechest
Vorschub:	Reach
Vorzüglich:	Excellent
Weich:	Soft
Weiss:	White
Werfen:	Whelped
Wesen:	Temperament
Wesenfest:	Firm temperament
Wesenscheu:	Shyness
Wetterfest:	Stormproof
Widerrist:	Withers
Zuchtbuch:	Stud book
Zuchtbuchnummer (SZ-NR):	Stud book number
Zuchter:	Breeder
Zuchtprüfung:	Approved (approval) as suitable for breeding

Classification Awards made by German Judges:

Vorzüglich Auslese (VA):	Excellent Selected – awarded only at the Siegerschau
Vorzüglich (V):	Excellent

Sehr Gut (SG):	Very Good
Gut (G):	Good
Ausreichend (A):	Satisfactory
Mangelhaft (M):	Poor
Ungenügend (U):	Unsatisfactory

Appendix E
Rottweiler Breed Clubs

The names and addresses of the current secretaries may be obtained from the Kennel Club, London.

The Rottweiler Club
The British Rottweiler Association
The Midland Rottweiler Club
The Northern Rottweiler Club
The Scottish Rottweiler Club
The Welsh Rottweiler Club
The Northern Ireland Rottweiler Club
The South Western Rottweiler Association
The Eastern Counties Rottweiler Club
London and South Eastern Rottweiler Club

Appendix F
Bibliography

The Rottweiler (translation), Hans Korn, 1939. Published by Colonial Rottweiler Club, USA.
  Written by the doyen of the breed, contains, apart from useful background information, a number of interesting photographs of the early Rottweilers.

Know Your Rottweiler (translation), D. Chardet, 1977. Published by Powderhorn Press. USA.
  Contains a considerable amount of original and stimulating thought on the breed.

Studies in the Breed History of the Rottweiler (translation), Manfred Schanzle, 1967. Published by Colonial and Medallion Rottweiler Clubs. USA.
  Written as a thesis for the degree of Doctor of Veterinary medicine, it contains a considerable amount of background information, much of it in the form of charts and graphs.

The Natural History of the Dog, R. & A. Fiennes, 1968. Published by Weidenfeld and Nicolson.
  Excellent background information on dogs in general.

Dogs of the World (translation), E. Schneider-Leyer, 1964. Published by Popular Dogs Publishing Co.
  Standard reference book giving brief details of virtually every breed in the world including some you may never have heard of.

All about Mating, Whelping and Weaning, David Cavell, 1981. Published by Pelham Books Ltd.
  Covers the whole subject very thoroughly including detailed photographs.

The Doglopaedia, J. M. Evans and Kay White, 1985. Published by Henston Ltd.
  Contains a massive amount of information of use to any dog owner. Slightly confusing although logical indexing in that it lists the problem rather than the cause.

Canine Terminology, Harold R. Spira, 1982. Published by Harper and Row. Australia.

Excellent glossary of technical and specialist terms used in connection with dogs.

My Friend Rik, Jan van Rheenen, 1960. Published by George G. Harrap.

Charming description of life with a Rottweiler.

Appendix G
The Unpopular Exhibitor

We have been unable to discover the origin of the following but consider that it encapsulates all those undesirable aspects of the show exhibitor. To its originator we offer our apologies for our inability to give the credit that is due.

HOW TO BECOME THE MOST UNPOPULAR EXHIBITOR

We have all met one – the exhibitor who has apparently never heard of the small courtesies that make showing enjoyable. It is doubtful if any one person has ever committed all the 'crimes' below, but we have all met more than one of them.

1. Arrive late, and be sure to park so that at least three other exhibitors (preferably long-distance) can't get out.

2. Leave at least one dog in the car with the windows closed.

3. Time things so that your party, complete with baggage, dogs, kids and Auntie Mabel, causes a traffic jam with the entrants trying to reach the ring for the first class.

4. If the benches on each side of you are not actually occupied by a dog, fill them up with your overflow of odds and ends . . .

5. . . . and become peevish if the rightful owner arrives and asks you to move them.

6. Make sure that your dog's benching chain is long enough to allow him to lunge out and intimidate passers-by . . .

7. . . . and if he can get his head round the partition and terrify the dog next door, so much the better.

8. Forget drinking vessel, so borrow someone else's bowl (without asking).

9. Provide the kids with candy-floss or little pink wafer biscuits and encourage them to feed the other exhibits.

10. Forget to exercise your dog, so that when nature finally does call, it does so in the most inconvenient place . . . like the middle of the ring.

11. When your class arrives, try to enter the ring whilst eating, half a pork pie for example, then throw this down, placed so that at least three dogs will compete for it. This is known as 'getting the ring on its toes'.

12. Light up a fag-end and puff smoke in the judge's face while he's examining your dog.

13. Converse with animation and volume with the ringside, especially about the judge.

14. Follow the Awful Exhibitors' Awards code: if you win, you indicate it was a foregone conclusion on account of the poor quality of the opposition. If second, you tear up your card. If third, you tear it up AND throw it over the left shoulder. If fourth, you do as for third, then jump on it. The warning should be given that by the time you get down to VHC or HC you may be in breach of the laws of decency. If not in the final line-up, you storm out, preferably kicking a chair.

15. When not in the ring, try and sit directly in front of the board where numbers of winners are exhibited, so that people have to ask you to move over so that they can copy down results. You can then snarl at them.

16. Try and leave as noticeably as possible, especially if unplaced. Preferably, trail the whole outfit straight across the ring when Best in Show is being judged.

17. You will, of course, have left the area around your bench knee-deep in waste with chewing gum stuck to the bench, water spilled, the other half of the pork pie trodden into the floor, and combings everywhere.

18. As a final gesture, you try and manoeuvre your car into a position where someone else has to be called out at an interesting point to move theirs.

When you get home, you announce that it was 'all a fiddle', 'the judge looked at the wrong end of the lead', and that you intend never to darken the doors of a dog show again.
    However, alas, you will . . . .

Index

187